C000254070

100
FOR AS
PRIMARY EDITION

CONTINUUM ONE HUNDREDS SERIES

100 IDEAS
FOR ASSEMBLIES

PRIMARY EDITION

Fred Sedgwick

continuum

For Mary and Peter Moore

Continuum International Publishing Group

The Tower Building   80 Maiden Lane
11 York Road   Suite 704
London   New York
SE1 7NX   NY 10038

www.continuumbooks.com

© Fred Sedgwick 2006

All rights reserved. No part of this publication may be reproduced
or transmitted in any form or by any means, electronic or
mechanical, including photocopying, recording, or any information
storage or retrieval system, without prior permission in writing from
the publishers.

Fred Sedgwick has asserted his right under the Copyright, Designs
and Patents Act, 1988, to be identified as Author of this work.

British Library Cataloguing-in-Publication Data
A catalogue record for this book is available from the British
Library.

ISBN: 0-8264-9101-4 (paperback)

Library of Congress Cataloging-in-Publication Data
A catalog record for this book is available from Library of Congress.

Typeset by Ben Cracknell Studios
Printed and bound in Great Britain by Ashford Colour Press Ltd,
Gosport, Hampshire

CONTENTS

ACKNOWLEDGEMENTS

Peggy Cotton
    (for permission to print poems by John Cotton)
Peter Moore
Sarah Parkinson
Emily Roeves
Chris Wardle

I have adapted material from the following books:

Ellen van Wolde, *Stories from the Beginning*, 1996,
    SCM Press.
William Darge, *Assembly Stories from Around the World*,
    1985, Oxford University Press.

Other material has been passed down orally or taken
from sources of traditional poetry and tales, and adapted
by the author. Every effort has been made to trace and
acknowledge copyright owners. Apologies are offered to
any author or copyright holder whose rights have been
unintentionally infringed. Due acknowledgement will be
made in subsequent editions on notification being made
to the publishers.

    Material marked by 'FS' is the author's own,
including all stories about Hannah and her
Grandfather.

What is an assembly? I'll try to answer that question in a paragraph or two. But first, what is an assembly not?

○ It is not a hymn, a prayer and a rollicking. I've been on the end of, seen – and indeed delivered – a few such threesomes. How the prayer (not to mention the hymn) contradicted the rollicking didn't bother me, whether as recipient, observant or deliverer.

○ It is not a 20-minute window for notices about the science club, the dance club or the choir.

○ It is not a run-through of a class's attempts at hitting a National Curriculum target (First Child: 'We have been learning about sieving.' Second Child: 'We have been learning about sieving'. . . and so on to the 27th child).

So what is an assembly? It is a chance:

○ to reinforce a sense of what it is to be part of a learning community.

○ to celebrate success within the school, and within the nation and around the world; and to console when individual, family, national or international events make us sad.

○ to open eyes to the unseen. A good assembly opens a window on what, because we are all busy, we are often blind to: the light that is inside every one of us.

Many of the best assemblies don't come out of books like this. For example, stories for the very young entrance sophisticates in Year 6. Read *Not Now Bernard* by David McKee, or *Where the Wild Things Are* by Maurice Sendak. *Amazing Grace* by Mary Hoffman is not only a brilliant story beautifully illustrated, but also an assembly about racism. On its own. No need for preaching.

Another source of assemblies might be the knowledge and enthusiasm of teachers who love their clog-dancing, their folk music, their oboe, their bird-watching. These enthusiasts have assemblies inside them, waiting to be shared with children.

But, notwithstanding all that, here are 100 ideas for assemblies. Most of them contain an element of surprise because many assemblies, and most books about assemblies, can be too predictable. This is boring. It can't be right to start the day, thereby setting its tone, by being dull!

Each assembly contains a prayer or meditation, or at least an opportunity for intense thinking. Sometimes this prayer, or meditation, or opportunity for intense thinking, is made explicit. Sometimes it is implicit.

Also, many of the assemblies ask the children to do something that can be fed into a later assembly: we want active learners. This is a principle of all these assemblies: teachers should do what you are asking the children to do.

For some of the assemblies I suggest the use of music. But because I don't care for assembly books that begin with a list of necessary things which, in my case, I do not have – the *Venus de Milo*, a cat, an old person – the music is never central to the assembly. You may not have the CD: fine. The music can be dispensed with.

But three further points about music. It is always a mistake to use lively music, of whatever kind – rock, jazz, classical – and then expect the children to sit still. The music should help everybody to achieve a reflective frame of mind. Keep it calm. Help everyone to listen. Cool it.

And it is disrespectful of the music itself, its composer and its performers to play it as a background while the children enter the hall. That's a general rule: silence is always better than music that has been chosen at random.

Some of the assemblies that follow lean towards the younger children and some towards the older ones. But nearly all are suitable for everyone.

Autumn/Winter

Music: A big splash is helpful here. Choose a piece with an impressive beginning, not played as the children come in, but when they are settled. The opening of Tchaikovsky's First Piano Concerto would be one of my choices.

Ask the children: 'How did you begin this day?' Collect responses. 'You woke up. What then?' Take answers about washing, dressing, breakfast, etc.

'What about the beginning of your life? You began as a baby. What did you do mostly?' Ask the children to respond. The children will talk about crawling, walking and early speech. You might suggest a mum or dad, or some other carer, would respond by saying something like: 'You "mewled and puked" in your parents' arms'!

How do you begin these:

o A football match
o A party
o A book
o A meal.

'Here are the beginnings of some books. Can you name them?' Have ready a range of books. Some should be recognizable for the very young. Some should be books that are recognizable by older children. I suggest:

o *Amazing Grace* by Mary Hoffman
o *Not Now Bernard* by David McKee
o *The Bible*
o Any *Harry Potter* book
o *His Dark Materials* by Philip Pullman.

Point out to the children how important a beginning is. That beginning a school year is important. That it is good to make sure that you are friends with everybody, as far as you can.

Meditation
Ask the children to close their eyes, then say: 'As we begin a school year, think of kind things we are going offer each other.'

End the assembly with a reprise of that big splash of music.

Music: The opening of 'Also Sprach Zarathustra' by Richard Strauss. If this isn't available, go for silence.

Tell the children that many people believe that the world began with a big bang. About 15 billion years ago, something tinier than a pin prick exploded, and in a few seconds there was a universe cooling down and getting ready for life: for you and me!

But other groups of people have different theories to explain the question of creation.

Ask the children: 'Has anyone made anything good lately?' They might say, a cake, a model, a painting . . .

Tell them the first Biblical story of the Creation, Genesis 1.1–2.4. I prefer the King James Bible, but you might prefer a modern version. Either way, read all of it, except for 'And the evening and the morning were the first/second/third [and so on] day', which you can coach the children in saying. This 'call and response' method of saying the words was, quite likely, how the passage was intended to be said in the Hebrew temple. Keeping the children involved in this way holds their attention.

Then produce something you have made or grown – a cake, a pot, a poem, a painting, a cushion cover, a house plant, a piano piece – and say: 'It may not be the best example of its kind in the world, but to me, it's good.' You might have asked another teacher to bring something as well.

Explain that people believe we were made like God ('in his image'), and that one way in which we are like God is that we can make good things. Tell the children that they are all going to make something today – perhaps more than one thing – that is good. It could be a well-done sum, a scientific experiment, a poem, a drawing, some gymnastics, a dance, a well-struck defensive header or a well-taken goal. Ask the children to close their eyes and think about something they can make today that will be good.

Tell the children that a poet called Dylan Thomas, when asked why he wrote poems, said something like this: 'I write poems for the pleasure of my friends, and to the glory of Almighty God, and I'd be a fool if I didn't.' Get them to repeat this after you, phrase by phrase.

Where Thomas talks here about poems, the same can be said for sums, scientific experiments, dances, defensive headers and goals.

Music: The opening of 'Also Sprach Zarathustra' by Richard Strauss. Or silence.

For today's assembly, everyone should bring in something good that they've made, or tell the story behind something good that they've made

One child from each class holds up his or her object – a painting, a poem, a model – or talks about a memory of, for example, a defensive header or a goal. Each child tells the rest of the school about it. Two or three of the teachers should have something to show as well.

Then you say: 'I want you all to show your object to someone else, or share your memory with them. And I want you to find something kind to say about what your friend has brought in. You should make sure you talk to someone from a different year. Then, in about three minutes, I will raise my right hand, and when you see my hand raised, or anyone else's, you will raise your hand and be silent.'

This last suggestion is a useful way of gaining silence without shouting. It always works, and works better as it becomes standard practice.

Repeat the Dylan Thomas quotation from Idea 2, with 'painting' or 'music' or something else in place of 'poems'.

To end with, here is a prayer:

Lord, I have made something. I am proud of it.
Help me today to make something I can be even more
proud of.
Amen

Music: The Strauss again – 'Also sprach Zarathustra' – though Hawaiian guitar music would also be suitable.

Tell the following story. It is set in the Pacific Ocean.

In the time of deep darkness, the god of creation threw a calabash* into the sky. It broke up, and bits of it became the sky, the sun, the moon and the earth. It was a mess, and it needed to be put in a kind of order. So the god of creation made a chief to rule the earth. To provide for the chief's needs, he filled the sea with good things.

> *Born was the coral,*
> *Born was the starfish,*
> *Born was the conch shell,*
> *Born was the fish,*
> *Born was the porpoise,*
> *Born was the shark in the sea there swimming . . .*

Adapted from Stories of the Beginning,
Ellen van Wolde

Ask the children to say 'Born was' whenever you point at them. You supply the rest of each line.

Tell the children: 'That's a poem from the middle of the Pacific Ocean.' Ask them: 'What is your favourite natural thing in the area where we live? Animal, bird, fish, flower, tree – it could be anything as long as it is natural. Now, close your eyes, and think of a sentence that begins "Born was . . ."'

Leave the room in silence for a minute. Then collect some of their suggestions.

Meditation
'Thank God for . . .' Then mention some of the natural things the children have suggested.

*A calabash is the skin of a gourd. A gourd is a large fleshy fruit.

In classrooms, before this assembly, ask everybody to complete the sentence, 'Born was . . .'. With younger children, a teacher or a learning assistant, can write it down for them. Then put the sentences up in the hall.

One school produced a 300-line poem (an epic!) that included the lines below. You could get the school to recite their poem in the manner described in Idea 4:

Born is the rainbow
Born is the sunlight on the sea
Born is the goat on the mountain
Born is the cat's purr when he smells his breakfast
Born is the baby's first smile
Born is my brother's smile when he scores a goal
Born is the moon shining on the water
Born is the smell of hyacinths
Born is the scent of my mum's perfume in the morning
Born is the sound of my father's jazz on the
    CD player.

OK, so the last two aren't, strictly, natural things. But be liberal. Be generous.

Then ask the children to say the poem that they have composed, in the same way.

Music: The Strauss again (see Idea 2).

Say to the children: 'Let's make up more lines beginning "Born was . . ." But this time, end these with things you can't see or touch.' Depending on the age and ability of the children, you could explain that these are 'abstract' things.

Start them off with a few lines of your own, or use these:

Born was the love of a boy for his baby sister
Born was peace in the world
Born was the joy of the summer
Born was the memory of lights in winter.

The children will almost certainly respond with one-word answers, for example, 'Born was happiness'. It is not difficult to help the children extend these lines with sensitive probing and questioning: 'Happiness when . . .?'

Once again, collect the lines the children offer and display them in the hall where they can be read during the days ahead. Ask the children to paint abstract pictures or to express in some other medium what they have written about in their lines.

Say 'Born was the world for us to take care of' and ask the children to close their eyes for half a minute. Say it again. Ask the children: 'What parts of the world can we take care of?'

Music: If there is some available, classical Chinese music would suit.

Present the following story:

The young man walked down the street. He was far from handsome. His teeth jutted over his lower lip. His nose was crooked. His eyes stared. He looked odd, even ugly. And, as people will, they called him names: 'Goofy', 'Stare-face', 'Ugly mug'.

So the young man stayed indoors. He read books. And when he did go out, he went to listen to the musicians in the Duke's music room.

Then he changed his life. He called on a master of music and asked to be taught how to play the zither*. The master looked at the clumsy young man's fat hands, and thought: 'He won't be any good! How will those sausage-like fingers work on the delicate strings?' But he was a kind master of music, and he welcomed the young man to his lessons.

For a week, the young man made a dreadful din, and finally the master decided that he'd had enough. 'Shall we try something else?' he asked. 'Oh no, Sir', replied the young man. 'I've got hold of the tune. Now I need to get hold of the rhythm.'

After another week, the master said 'That's enough practice with rhythm now. Shall we go on to something else?' 'Oh no, Sir', replied the young man. 'I've got hold of the tune, and I've got hold of the rhythm. Now I must get hold of the mood of the music.'

Again, the master listened in pain to the sounds the young man made with the zither. 'You must have had enough of the mood of the music now,' he said. 'Let's move on to something else.' 'Oh no, Sir,' said the young man. 'I have got hold of the tune and the rhythm and the mood. Now I want to get hold of – no – I must try to understand – the man who made this music.'

The master let him play for a long time. The music gradually began to sound better. Then, one day, the

---

*A zither is a musical instrument with between 30 and 40 strings, and has to be play with great dexterity.

9

young man smiled. 'I know who wrote this music. He
was a great man. He was the great King Wen, of the
olden times.'

'You are right,' said the master. 'King Wen did
indeed write this music.'

The ugly, stumbling young man was Confucius, who was
born in China in the autumn 400 years before the birth
of Christ. He said this (ask the children to close their
eyes and cover them with their hands, and say, slowly):

Be careful of these things:
Your eyes, so you can see;
Your ears, so you may learn;
Your face, so that you may always reflect kindness;
Your manners, so that you may show respect;
Your words, so that they may be true;
Your dealings with other people, so that they are
*   always fair.*

Confucius' motto was this:

Don't do to other people what you wouldn't want them
to do to you.

Not a bad motto for our school! Can you think of some
things that you wouldn't want other people to do to you?
Or can you think of a better motto?

Remind the children of Confucius' motto from assembly Idea 7:

Don't do to other people what you wouldn't want them to do to you.

Ask the children to make a list: 'Things you don't want done to you'. They might give the following:

○ You don't want to be bullied.
○ You don't want someone to push in front of you in the lunch queue.
○ You don't want anyone to call you names.

These are things we don't want done to us, and so we won't do them to others.

Then turn the motto around. Not, 'Don't do to other people what you wouldn't want them to do to you', but 'Do unto others what you would like them to do to you'.

What would you like someone to do to you today?

○ Ask you to join in a game when you're on your own.
○ Help you up when you've fallen over.

We must do these things to other people.

Meditation
TWO BOYS

He was angry, so others were angry to him.
He was sharp with his tongue, so others were sharp
*   with their tongues to him.*
He was free with his arms and legs, punching and
*   kicking and pushing, so others were free with their*
*   ams and legs to him.*

He is generous with his time and feelings, so others are
*   generous to him.*
He picks up the child on the playground, so when he
*   falls, others pick him up.*
He puts others first, so others put him first.

FS

11

Music: Something instrumental.

You need CDs for this assembly. The music should help children and teachers to reflect. Choose something instrumental, not vocal. One of the aims is to train the children's ears to listen. The other (connected) aim is to encourage children to appreciate music. Ask the children to close their eyes and prepare to listen. Tell them that William Blake, the poet and artist, said that we should look at something 'until it hurts'. We should listen to something until it hurts, as well. Then play the music, just a minute of it.

Here are some suggestions for the music:

○ 'Blue Horizon' by Sidney Bechet
○ The second movement of Schubert's String Quintet
○ The slow movement (the second) of Tchaikovsky's First Piano Concerto.

Whatever you choose, it should be music that you are fond of. Or better, passionate about.

Challenge the children:

○ 'What instruments can you hear?'
○ 'Describe the speed (introduce the word 'tempo') of the music.'
○ 'What is the mood of the music?'

Other teachers should be primed to play a favourite instrumental piece. Ask the children to listen, hard, again. They can't listen, or look, hard enough . . . Ask the children: 'What is your favourite music?' Then say this psalm, which is about music, with the older children saying 'Praise him' when you point at them. Call and response again! The last 'Praise him' should be a shout.

Praise him.
    Praise ye the Lord.
Praise him.
    Praise him with the sound of the trumpet.
Praise him.
    Praise him with the harp and the guitar.

Praise him.
>Praise him with drums and dance, and with
>violins and organs.

Praise him.
>Praise him on the cymbals.

>Let everything that has breath praise the Lord.

Praise him.

Psalm 150, adapted from the Authorized Version

'Now let's praise him, by singing . . .' This is one
assembly where a song or hymn is necessary. And
perhaps some children could sing or play music for the
whole school.

THE CHILDREN'S FAVOURITE MUSIC

Music: Something you played for Idea 9. Repeat the psalm from Idea 9, in the same way.

This assembly establishes a principle that is relevant throughout this book: that children should, wherever possible, take part in assemblies. In other words, some of the assemblies should be theirs as much as yours.

This assembly is composed of pieces of music, one chosen by a child in each class. The music will probably be mostly vocal. The children should be told to think, before making a final decision, about the following:

○ Will I always like this music?
○ Why do I like it?
○ What instruments can I hear in it?
○ Where did I first hear this music?

The children should have rehearsed their comments.

Ask the rest of the children the same questions as those you asked in Idea 9, about the tempo, the instruments and the mood. Then repeat Psalm 150.

The point of this repetition is fourfold: to hear a great, ancient, religious text; to become familiar with it; to become familiar, too, with good prose; and to see the importance of music to an ancient people, the Jews of King David's time.

An assembly shouldn't always be about the humanities, or artistic or religious matters. We should celebrate the whole curriculum. Lead this assembly with a class of children with whom you have practised.

Show the school drawings of shapes: rectangles, including squares; triangles, isosceles, equilateral, right-angled; circles, ovals.

Ask the children: 'How many of these shapes can you see in the hall?' There will, most obviously, be rectangles in the windows. Ask them to look at the windows. How many rectangles can they count? Are there any circles? Then encourage the children to look for other shapes. There may be triangles in the roof, for example.

Talk about all the shapes that the children can see. Ask the prepared class to form:

o A circle
o An oval
o A square
o An equilateral triangle.

Say to the children: 'Go about school today, and the playground, and the field, looking for shapes.'

THE FIRST SNOWY DAY

Music: Any wintry music, for example, 'Winter' from Vivaldi's 'Four Seasons', or Prokoviev's 'Sleigh Ride', or, rather less elevated, 'Winter Wonderland'.

Bring in some snow. Show it to the children, and leave it in a bowl hidden behind a screen. It will, of course, melt as the assembly progresses.

Meanwhile, read these:

THREE LITTLE POEMS FOR WINTER

1

Icing on earth's cake –
underneath there's fruit
waiting for birth.

2

The garden is a perfect page.
Let's print on it now
with boots and sledge-rails.

3

Look at the hedge!
The white speckled hedge!
And that robin in there, hunting.

All by FS

Point out that each one contains metaphors: snow as icing, earth underneath as a cake, snowy grass as a blank page.

Ask the children: when they're out at playtime or lunchtime, could they spend two minutes looking at something wintry – such as snow, a twig, a bare tree, the sky, a cloud, a fence covered with snow, frost, ice – and compose a poem about it with 1, 2 or 3 lines only. Could they write it down as soon as they get back to class?

Some of them will manage metaphors. Encourage the children to draw a picture to go with it. Finally, look at the snow you brought in, now melted. Could somebody write a tiny poem about what this snow looks like now?

Read the poems the children wrote after the first snowy day. Read a winter story. Oscar Wilde's 'The Selfish Giant' is a brilliant one. It ends with one of the most perfect sentences in English: 'And when the children ran into the garden that afternoon, they found the giant lying dead under the tree, all covered with white blossoms'.

Also good for reading during winter is the chapter in *The Lion, the Witch and the Wardrobe* by C S Lewis when the witch is carrying Edmund in her sledge.

> *'Always winter and never Christmas' – what an awful notion!*

Meditation

> *Always snow and no tree*
> *And if there's a tree, no lights on it*
> *And no presents under it.*
> *Dark all day*
> *And no bright light to look forward to.*

> *FS*

Ask the children to come up with a meditation on this model: 'Always winter and never Christmas'. In one school, children came up with:

> *Always cold, and no Jesus.*
> *Always darkness, never a star.*
> *Always hate, and no love.*

IDEA 14

Music: Indian music, if available.

All the religious assemblies should, if possible, be followed by an assembly led by a member of the relevant religious group.

This is an assembly about Guru Nanak, who founded the Sikh religion.

There was a boy called Nanak. When he grew up, he went to work for a rich man. He was his accountant: he had to keep a check on the man's money, how he was earning it, how he was spending it, whether people who owed him money were paying him on time. He was good at his job.

But it wasn't much fun looking after account books in dark rooms when there was bright warm sunlight outside. Nanak preferred wandering around the countryside. He was especially fond of the water.

One day he was swimming in the river. As the rich man watched him from the bank, Nanak disappeared. The rich man waited for Nanak's head to reappear, but it didn't.

The rich man hired divers, and they searched the bottom of the river. Fishermen dragged their nets. But the boy was nowhere to be found. Everybody assumed that he must be drowned.

But three days later, he returned home. Without speaking to anyone, he began to carry food and drink out. He went into the street, and gave rice, meat and drink to the poor people who had almost nothing.

When he was in the river, he explained, he had seen a vision, and now he had to preach God's message.

He was the Guru Nanak, the founder of Sikhism. Part of his message was:

> *There is no Hindu. There is no Muslim. I am a brother to all who love God, and all lovers of God are brothers together.*

Tell the children that this is like something the Christian St Paul wrote: 'In Christ there is no Greek or Jew, no

A SIKH STORY FOR NOVEMBER OR DECEMBER

18

male or female'. Both for Guru Nanak and for St Paul, every human being is worthy of the love of God.

Ask the children: 'Does anyone know anything more about the life of the Guru Nanak?' Ask the children to close their eyes, and cover them with their hands. Then say the words of Guru Nanak:

If I had a hundred thousand tongues, not just one
And a hundred thousand times twenty
I'd say, and say, and say again
There is but one God, and only one.

Preparation: This is an atypical assembly in this book because you will need some props. But a large onion, brought from home, bought on the way to work, begged or pilfered from the school kitchen is not difficult to find.

You will also need a knife and a plate. I must state the obvious – health, safety – keep the knife out of pupils' reach!

Show the onion to the children and ask them what it is. Tell them that this onion is just like a story, and you are going to explain why. Cut the onion in half. A good story has:

o Layers – ideas develop and interconnect, getting deeper. Pull away some of the skin layers from the onion.

o Surprises – twists and turns which we might not expect. See how, as the reddish-brown skin is pulled away, the twists and turns in the onion reveal a pure white interior and a pattern.

o Structure – stories have a structure which brings the reader back to the beginning. They have a circular logic, ending where the story began, just like the rings from the onion. (Cut off a slice to show the onion rings.)

o Strength – a good story has strong ideas, just like the onion has strong smells. Allow some children to smell it, and get them to describe the smell to everyone else. And, just as when you chop onions they can make you cry, so too can a powerful story. It can make you cry with laughter, joy or sadness.

An onion, like a story, goes with other things. You can't eat an onion on its own, you have to combine it with other ingredients, cook it and serve it. Just as with a good story, you need to think about it, savour it in your mind and then share it with someone else by telling them about it, or recommending that they read it.

So an onion really is rather like a good story! Ask the children, What is their favourite story? Ask them about the surprises in it.

This assembly is about two things:

○ Stories
○ How to tell them so that your audience stays listening. This means clearly, and with expression.

If this assembly is delivered early in the school year, it will improve, at a stroke, the children's contributions to all subsequent assemblies. But the messages in it need to be reinforced throughout the year. It is a chance to teach children about techniques of reading aloud to other children:

○ Reading aloud is not about shouting.
○ They should open the mouth wide as they speak.
○ They should be aware of speaking from the diaphragm, not the throat.
○ They should be aware of breathing deeply and regularly, to give their voice power.
○ They should hold the script in a position that neither covers their mouth, nor forces them to look down.
○ They should make as much eye contact as possible with their audience.

A child from every year, coached in these rules, should be prepared to talk about his or her favourite story, and some of them should be prepared to read it, or have it read, to the whole school.

You could also ask two teachers to tell their favourite stories. Obviously, they will be aware of, and will practise, the rules given above.

TELLING A STORY WELL

This is the first of seven stories about Hannah and her Grandfather.

Grandfather began by not liking Hannah. Eight years ago, she was a brand new human being, just out of the wash, but he said she looked like an old man.

And she did. Her eyes were cross. Her face was wrinkled and red, like an apple beginning to rot.

But a little while later, Grandfather saw how beautiful she was. He used to cradle her in his arms, and sing her songs about love. 'You are my sunshine,' he used to sing, softly. 'My only sunshine . . .'

Hannah's Dad knew he was thinking about his wife. Hannah's Grandma had died, long before Hannah was born. 'Grace would have loved her,' he used to say, half to them, half to himself.

He loved taking her out in her buggy. He used to show her the ducks in the park. He threw bits of bread, and Hannah watched the ducks flock around her and peck at each other, and she laughed when they made their quacking noises.

Hannah wasn't always lovely. She used to crease up her face and yell. She used to yell and yell for a long time. Grandfather used to frown when she did this.

'What a noise that baby makes!' he used to say.

One day, Hannah yelled for so long that her Dad became worried.

Grandfather was worried too, but he took the baby Hannah in his arms.

She cried for a while more. Then she looked into Grandfather's eyes.

And Grandfather's eyes looked into hers. He sang, very softly, 'You are my sunshine . . .' Then he added, quietly: 'My only sunshine . . .'

And she stopped crying.

And Grandfather stopped worrying.

And Hannah's Dad stopped worrying too.

And Grandfather gave her a drink from her bottle of warm milk, and kissed her on her forehead.

FS

Ask the children:

- ○ You must have heard – what horrible things did you do when you were a baby?!
- ○ Who looked after you?
- ○ And what about love? You think someone's horrible, but it turns out that they are beautiful . . .
- ○ Can you think of a sentence about a baby brother or sister that goes like this: I love you Hannah, although sometimes you scream and shout?

The staff should be primed to write a sentence like this about their classes, or individuals in their classes:

- ○ I love you children even though you drop your coats on the floor.
- ○ I love you Rory even though you support Manchester United.

Ask the children to close their eyes: 'Please think of someone you are fond of, and of something kind you are going to do for them today.'

LITTLE THINGS

Music: Anything quiet played by a solo instrument.

Preparation: Bring in some little things: a cogwheel, a pair of toddler's shoes, a stone, a cup of tea.

This assembly is about how important little things are. Tell the children: 'To know what the ocean tastes like, you don't have to drink it all. It takes only one mouthful.'

Tell the children: 'Think about the little parts in an engine . . . the cog looks like nothing, but without it the car wouldn't go. A toddler's first pair of shoes is a big event in their life. A stone has existed for millions of years. I can't come to work without my first cup of tea.'

The poet William Blake knew about the importance of little things. He could see 'a World in a Grain of Sand, And a Heaven in a Wild Flower'. The great dictionary-maker and writer, Dr Samuel Johnson, told his friend to write down all the little things in his life: 'It is by studying little things that we attain the great knowledge of having as little misery and as much happiness as possible.'

Take a stone and say, 'This stone has been on my desk for twenty years, with its cool weight in my palm, with the faint smell of rainy mornings.'

Or you could take a leaf 'that I've just picked up outside the school gate.'

Or 'Look at my grown-up son's first pair of shoes, the soles are hardly worn.'

Ask the children: 'Can you find something little? Can you put it here in the hall so that we can talk about it tomorrow?'

Play the music: a solo track, or maybe the pianist can play a simple tune, representing a little thing that we can hear.

Music: Anything quiet played by a solo instrument.

This is an assembly mainly for KS1. But KS2 love it too.

The children come into the hall and look at the little things they have brought in (see Idea 18). Then tell a story: often the smallest things we own – a ring, a necklace, a photo in our wallet or pencil case – are the most precious. Here is a story about one girl, Hannah, and something – or someone? – tiny.

A BOOK ABOUT TEDDY SMALL

Hannah has lost Teddy Small.

She is looking everywhere, because Teddy Small is her favourite teddy.

She looks in the cupboard under the stairs. She looks behind the vacuum cleaner. She looks in all the shoes. She looks in the garden. She looks in the hedge. She goes upstairs.

Is Teddy Small in the cupboard under the stairs?

No, he isn't.

Is he in the garden?

No, he isn't.

Is he upstairs?

No, he isn't.

Hannah looks beside her seat in the car. There is Dopey Dog and Hannah's favourite book. There is a half-eaten biscuit.

But no Teddy Small.

Hannah stares out of the window. She feels sad.

She hears a loud noise coming from the bathroom. What is going on?

Some of the other teddies and some of the dolls are playing football. They kick and head and shout. They jump and cheer and sing loud songs.

Hannah looks hard for Teddy Small. Is he there at the football match?

No, she can't see him.

Hannah asks the referee if he has seen Teddy Small. No, he hasn't.

Hannah stares at the floor. She feels sad.

Hannah hears another loud noise. This one is coming from the landing.

*Some of the dolls and some of the teddies are
playing records and dancing to the music.*

*Hannah looks hard for Teddy Small. Is he there at
the dance?*

No, he isn't.

*Hannah asks the disc jockey if she has seen Teddy
Small.*

*No, she hasn't seen him. Hannah stares at the book
shelves. She feels sad.*

*She hears another loud noise coming from the
kitchen.*

*Some dogs and cats are chasing round and round.
Rabbits hop and skid on the shiny floor. A kangaroo is
leaping round the legs of the kitchen table.*

*Hannah looks hard for Teddy Small. Is he here
among all this rumpus?*

No, she can't see him.

*Is he helping the rabbits to hop and skid and slide?
No, he isn't.*

*She asks the kangaroo if she has seen Teddy Small.
No, she hasn't seen him.*

Hannah stares at the mirror. She feels sad.

*Teddy Small is her favourite teddy. Where can he be?
She sits down in the living room.*

It is quiet in here after all the noise.

*Hannah looks at the carpet near the wall. There is
Teddy Small behind a chair. He is reading a book.*

'Hello Teddy Small!'

*Hannah picks him up and holds him tight. She says:
'What is that book about?'*

The book is about a girl called Hannah.

Hannah has lost Teddy Small.

But now she's found him.

FS

The above story is based on the story in the next
assembly, Idea 20.

Music: Anything played quietly by a solo instrument.

Thomas Hardy was a poet and a novelist, and he said this was his favourite story in the Bible. If possible, it would be good to sing 'Dear Lord and Father of mankind' here, because it is based on this story.

> *There was a teacher called Elijah. The people would not listen to him. In fact, they had become angry with him because he told the truth, and they didn't want to hear the truth. So he went away, and sat alone in a cave.*
>
> *God said to him, 'Elijah, what are you doing here?' Elijah told God that the people would not listen to him. They didn't want to know the truth. They were trying to kill him.*
>
> *God told him to stand on the mountain. And a great wind came, tearing the mountain and breaking the rocks. Elijah listened. But God wasn't in the great wind.*
>
> *And there was an earthquake, and the ground shook. But God wasn't in the earthquake.*
>
> *And there was a fire, burning like great scarlet and yellow flowers. But God wasn't in the fire.*
>
> *And there was a still small voice.*
>
> *[Pause]*
>
> *Elijah listened.*
>
> *[Pause]*
>
> *And God was in the still small voice.*

Ever since humankind was born, people have listened for the voice of God. Let's listen for a still small voice in our hall now.

Think for a moment in the silence: where's the best place to listen for the voice of God? And if you heard the voice of God, what would want to say to him?

Collect some suggestions: on a beach, in a wood, in the sanctuary of a church, or a mosque, or a temple, or a synagogue, in a bedroom, under the stairs . . . One good place to hear God's voice is in your own head.

Remind the children of the story about Hannah (Idea 19). It is based on this Bible story.

THE STILL SMALL VOICE – AN ASSEMBLY BASED ON 1 KINGS 19.11–13

This assembly is about making the best of the world's resources.

Bring into the hall as much household rubbish as you can find: bottles, glass and plastic; newspapers and magazines; cans; old clothes and shoes; garden waste. Arrange it so it is jumbled together.

Then ask a group of children (one from each year? a group of Year 6s?) to come to the front and to arrange the rubbish into sets, putting like with like. They should, of course, wear plastic gloves. They should then display the rubbish as attractively as possible.

Ask the children: 'Where will each set go?', 'What will it be used for?'

o Glass will be used to make more bottles, or used in building and road materials.
o Plastic can be made into fleece jackets, traffic cones, street furniture and the like.
o Paper will make more paper.
o Cans will . . .
o Clothes will . . .
o Shoes will . . .
o Garden waste will . . .

The local waste management service is almost certain to be able to send someone to talk to the children, and to answer these questions. But first, the children could find out themselves, perhaps using the Internet during a session in the ICT room.

For this assembly the children and staff should come into the hall with curtains closed and lights off. Perhaps even the heating could be turned off. There is no music. You are looking to create a cold, dark, barren atmosphere. It would be perfect, but not necessary, if the staff and children could be arranged in a rectangle, with you in the space in the middle. Then, in a quiet voice, tell this story:

> *It is winter at the beginning of the world. The first snow falls, and the people shiver in the bitter cold. They begin to starve because they cannot cook. All the fire is in heaven, where the gods keep it to themselves.*
>
> *Prometheus, who lives in the heavens with the gods, looks down on the shivering, hungry people and feels sorry for them. He comes down from the heavens and puts a green fennel leaf into the hottest volcano on Earth. It flames like a brilliant scarlet flower. He takes the fire to the people, and . . .*

Someone lights a candle here, as large a one as possible. Then someone else opens the curtains and puts on the lights, as suddenly as possible. The heating whirrs. Continue the story.

> *They become warm. They learn how to cook. They grow in intelligence. With fire comes civilization, or 'enlightenment', light in darkness, villages, towns, farming, books, art, music . . .*

Ask the children: 'What else comes with civilization?'

Ask them: 'What could the people not do before Prometheus gave them fire? What could they do, once he had given them fire?'

Ask them, when they get back to their classes, to think of words to describe fire: its colours, its shapes, the good things it does, the bad things it does . . . Collect their thoughts for another assembly. If they have time, they could paint pictures, as abstract as they like, of fire.

Restrict their choice of colours to reds, yellows, oranges and whites.

CANDLES

Preparation: Close any curtains and make the room dark.

Set large candles – as many as possible – in the darkened room. Ask the children to look at them closer in turns. What could you call the candle flame? Give it a name. You might tell them that one child in another school called it these things:

> My candle is my Way finder
> And my Light bearer
> My flame is my Path to God
> And a Light maker
> It is my Wax burner
> And my Bird of light
> It is my Feather of fire
> My Night dancer
> It is a Dancing flame
> My Torch of freedom
> It is a Darkness fighter
> And the Lighter of the world
> It is my Light of the room
> My Animal of fire
> It is Lighting darkness
> And a Fire tongue
> It is the Messenger to God
> And the Path to freedom.

These are called kennings. A kenning is a 'way of calling something' (in adult terms, an epithet). Could each class spend five minutes collecting candle kennings?

Then ask: 'What are candles for?' Light, of course. For religious reasons, they are for:

o Paschal candle, used by Jews to celebrate Passover, and Christians to celebrate Easter.
o Menorahs, used by Jews to celebrate the winter festival, Hanukkah.

Local clergy might be able to lend examples of these. Consider candles in other religions, and scented candles.

But candles are also beautiful, which is why many of us put them on the table for special meals: birthdays, anniversaries and religious festivals, for example.

Ask a child whose birthday it is to come out to the front (assuming he or she is not shy) and say these verses, with the child's name in the gaps.

SONG FOR A BIRTHDAY

Is it raining outside? Is it snowing?
Is the sun shining bright in the sky?
Is it foggy or grey? Is today a bright day?
It's a very good day. This is why,

Well,

Today is _____'s birthday
And everyone gathers to say
'Today is _____'s birthday,
_____'s own special day'.

Is it pizza for lunch? Or spaghetti?
Is it chips? Is it cheese? Is it beans?
Is it curry and rice? (Yes, that would be nice)
It's _____'s day, and that means

That

Today is _____'s birthday
And everyone gathers to say
'Today is _____'s birthday,
_____'s own special day'.

Is it maths? Is it English, or music?
Is it history? Science? PE?
It's _____'s day, it's a simply great day,
For her/him, and for you, and for me

'Cos

Today is _____'s birthday
And everyone gathers to say
'Today is _____'s birthday,
_____'s own special day'.

FS

This assembly can be used as an addition to any other assembly.

A BIRTHDAY ASSEMBLY

Another idea for a child's birthday: ask his or her classmates to make a list of his or her good qualities, and read them out to the school.

Some research should show whether a child's birthday is also a famous national or international anniversary. Link the child with that anniversary.

Preparation: Give this assembly on 4 November (not 5 November: the day before gives an opportunity for the necessary safety word).

Everybody knows that, in the UK, we light bonfires and set off fireworks at this time of the year. But who knows why? Ask for responses.

The Catholics in England hated the King, James I, about as much as he hated the Catholics. They did not believe him to be a true king, because he was a Protestant. As so often, we see that believers in the same religion do not always get on. Both Catholics and Protestants are Christians, but they can be hateful to each other.

In November 1605, Robert Catesby, a Catholic, and a small band of men, including Guy Fawkes, hired a cellar underneath the Parliament buildings. They filled it with 20 barrels of gunpowder, and camouflaged it with wood.

At the moment the King sat on the throne in the rooms above, Guy Fawkes was to light a fuse and the whole place was to be blown into the sky, killing the King and all his ministers.

But one of the plotters had betrayed them, and had told the King's ministers about the plan. At the moment when Fawkes was about to light the gunpowder, boots thumped on the stone floor outside the cellar. The door flew open, smashing against the wall. Soldiers charged in. Holding a lantern up to Fawkes' face, while the others grabbed his arms and held them against his back, one of them cried, 'I arrest you, traitor, in the name of the King!'

Fawkes was dragged away and tortured until he gave the soldiers the names of the other conspirators. Some died when they tried to escape. Others, including Fawkes, were executed.

Meditation

A prayer for tolerance:

> *God, make us aware that all religions are searching for truth. Help us to respect each other's version of that truth.*

GUY FAWKES

Remember Guy Fawkes. And remember your safety. And remember that my cat (or dog, or similar!) is frightened for about three weeks this time of year because the banging of fireworks goes on and on and on . . .

Music: 'Mars', from *The Planet Suite* (Holst).

Preparation: A large reproduction of *Guernica*, by Picasso.

This is an assembly for mid-November, when Remembrance Day occurs. Begin by discussing fights in the school playground. What causes them? In the silent hall, ask the children to close their eyes and cover them with their hands. Collect responses.

THE FIGHT

There's a fight on the playground today –
Two big boys from Mr Magee's

Are knocking the daylights out of each other
Under the trees.

The girls are silent and staring
And Clare whispers 'Stop it, Paul'

As the fighting gets wilder and feet jab out
And fingers maul.

I watch, and I'm glad it's not Joe
And me in that horrible space –

Not my stomach winded, not my nose bleeding,
Not my burning face.

The sky is bright. Two planes fly
Out from the base, while one

Boy holds the other down with his knee
And breathes, 'You done?'

There's a fight on the playground today –
Paul Topple from Mr Magee's

Is crushing the daylights out of John Randall
Under the trees.

FS

I wonder what those planes are going off to do? Fights between nations are wars. Ask the children:
    'What does the soldier say about war?'

- One soldier from WW1 said, 'Some people say, my mates gave their lives. They didn't. My mates didn't give their lives; their lives were taken away from them.'
- One Russian soldier said, 'Three quarters of a soldier's life is spent in aimlessly waiting about.'
- Another old soldier from WW2 said, 'When I remember the war I think of the smell of burning tyres.'
- What does the soldier's lady – wife, girlfriend, sister, mother – say about war? What does the soldier's family say?
- One woman, whose young husband fought in WW2, said to me, 'When he went away again after leave, we were both thinking that we might never see each other again.'
- What does the soldier's father, or his little brother, say about war? What do other people say?
- What does the general say about war?
- What does the man who makes the guns, bombs and missiles say about war?
- What does the child say about war?
- What do the people remembering say about war?
- What do you say about war?

Bring in a newspaper, and read a story from a war front.

Meditation
A prayer for peace.

> *Lord, make me an instrument of thy peace.*
> *Where there is hatred, let me sow love.*
> *Where there is injury, pardon.*
> *Where there is discord, union.*
> *Where there is doubt, faith.*
> *Where there is despair, hope.*
> *Where there is darkness, light.*
> *Where there is sadness, joy . . .*
> *Lord, make me an instrument of thy peace.*

Music: A Vera Lynn song, such as 'Keep the Home Fires Burning'.

I was at a school where I was asked to help the children to write poems about World War II. They did this with the help of the repeating line 'I am the man/woman/child, etc. who . . .', and some powerful images of battle, evacuation and bombed towns, their own in particular, that were displayed on the wall.

Here are some examples of what they wrote, which you could read to the children:

o I am the woman who loved the man who died in the battle, and now I have only memories . . .
o I am the child who went away with my gas mask, because of the bombs, and I didn't like it . . .
o I am the man who lies still on the battlefield . . .
o I am the girl in the photo in the dead soldier's wallet . . .

Our assembly, which took place at the end of the day, lasted an hour. Fifty people came, the oldest 96 years old, bussed in from homes in the area. The children served them tea and sandwiches. There was a group of singers singing WW2 songs, and a Winston Churchill impersonator read some of the famous speeches.

The children and the old people seemed to be equally entranced by all this (and each other). The old people listened attentively as the children read the poems that they'd written with me in the morning.

If there is an old people's home nearby, I recommend approaching its residents. Invite the men and women to tea and sandwiches. The children will learn about them as individuals, and they will learn about the old people.

More generally, assemblies should sometimes include members of the community from outside the school.

Tell the children that the Chinese have a word that translates as 'respect for the old'. There is no word for this in English. Why might that be?

THE PRINCE

Preparation: A chipped cup.

There was an Indian prince whose family kept him from pain and death. He was not free to wander from the palace grounds, and only handsome people were allowed to be his servants. He saw only beautiful flowers. He ate only perfect fruit. Nothing that was broken, nothing that was spoiled, was allowed anywhere near him. So he never drank from a chipped cup, like this one. [Hold yours up.]

But, every year, the prince took part in a procession through the city. One day he saw a sick man, lying still on the road. Another day he saw an old woman, her arms like withered twigs. And another day he saw a dead man.

He asked 'What has happened to these people?' But no one in his family would tell the prince about those men and the women, who were so unlike any other people he had ever seen. They troubled him. His family rushed him on.

He thought that there was much to be learned about in the world outside his palace. And he left his beautiful home. He slipped out with a servant when no one else was awake. When he was a long way from the palace, he swapped clothes with the servant, and gave him all his jewels, and said goodbye.

He thought he would find truth by giving up his luxuries. He lived in the forest on a grain of rice a day. But soon, of course, he became ill. He was found by a woodcutter's daughter, who took him to her house and nursed him and made him better. He had learned something: that there was a way between richness and poverty, a middle way. In this middle way, he began to understand the world.

He understood that life is often painful, and that it doesn't last long. He understood, too, that we bring most of the pain upon ourselves by being greedy, selfish and ignorant. He became a Buddha. Others came to learn from him, and today 2,500 years later, he has millions of followers all over the world, looking for the middle way, helping others and trying to understand the world. Perhaps we could learn from Prince Siddhartha, as well.

Here is something Prince Siddhartha used to say. Say each phrase after me:

Three things cannot be hidden:
the sun,
the moon
and the truth.

This is an assembly mainly for KS1, but KS2 love it too.
There is no message in this assembly.

Hannah has grown up a little . . .

HANNAH'S WINTER STORY

*Hannah ran out into the snowy garden in her
knickers. She saw the snowman she had built with
Grandfather the night before. Grandfather said:*

'*That can't be right.*
You look a sight.
Don't be so bold.
You'll catch a cold.
Come here now!'

*Hannah ran out into the snowy garden in her knickers
and vest. Grandfather said:*

'*That can't be right.*
You look a sight.
Don't be so bold.
You'll catch a cold.
Back in the house.'

*Hannah ran out into the snowy garden in her
knickers, her vest and her tartan trousers. Grandfather
said:*

'*That can't be right.*
You look a sight.
Don't be so bold.
You'll catch a cold.
Indoors, please.'

*Hannah ran out into the snowy garden in her
knickers, her vest, her tartan trousers and her football
shirt that was blue and white (Come on you Blues!***).*
Grandfather said:

---

*These are the colours of my team, Ipswich Town. Obviously, you
will substitute the colours of the local team. Ask for the children's
suggestions.

'That can't be right.
You look a sight.
Don't be so bold.
You'll catch a cold.
Please Hannah, my dear.'

Hannah ran out into the snowy garden in her
knickers, her vest, her tartan trousers, her football shirt
that was blue and white (Come on you Blues!) and
her woolly jumper. Grandfather said:

'That can't be right.
You look a sight.
Don't be so bold.
You'll catch a cold.
Here, now, sweetheart.'

Hannah ran out into the snowy garden in her
knickers, her vest, her tartan trousers, her football shirt
that was blue and white (Come on you Blues!), her
woolly jumper and her red wellington boots (she'd left
her socks inside her boots, all bunched up and a wee bit
smelly, so she put them on too). Grandfather said:

'That can't be right.
You look a sight.
Don't be so bold.
You'll catch a cold.
Hannah, darling.'

Hannah ran out into the snowy garden in her
knickers, her vest, her tartan trousers, her football shirt
that was blue and white (Come on you Blues!), her
woolly jumper and her red wellington boots (she'd left
her socks inside her boots, all bunched up and a wee bit
smelly, so she put them on too). And she put on her
coat. Grandfather said:

'That can't be right.
You look a sight.
Don't be so bold.
You'll catch a cold.
Wear this, my love.'

*Hannah ran out into the snowy garden in her
knickers, her vest, her tartan trousers, her football shirt
that was blue and white (Come on you Blues!), her
woolly jumper and her red wellington boots (she'd left
her socks inside her boots, all bunched up and a wee bit
smelly, so she put them on too). And she put on her
coat and her football scarf (blue and white).
Grandfather said,*

*'That can't be right.
You look a sight.
Don't be so bold.
You'll catch a cold.
Come here, my angel.'*

*Hannah ran out into the snowy garden in her
knickers, her vest, her tartan trousers, her football shirt
that was blue and white (Come on you Blues!), her
woolly jumper, and her red wellington boots (she'd left
her socks inside her boots, all bunched up and a wee bit
smelly, so she put them on too). And she put on her
coat and her football scarf (blue and white) and her
bobble hat. Yes, her bobble hat was blue and white.
And Grandfather said:*

*'That's right.
Pull that scarf on tight.
And here are your gloves.'*

*And Hannah and Grandfather threw snowballs at the
snowman in the winter morning light.*

FS

What winter games do you like to play? Collect some
responses from the children.

Preparation: An orange, a lime (if possible), a lemon, sums (as shown below) written large on a card (or projected using an OHP), a large zero, a pair of pyjamas, a piece of cotton and a bottle of beer (if you allow beer in school).

'What do all these things have in common?' No one will know, almost certainly, unless you have an expert in etymology in the hall.

Tell the children that the words for these things – 'alcohol' in the case of the beer – all come from Arabic. They are words that Muslims have given to the world. Some of them are older than the Muslim religion, but they all came to us through Muslims: through Islam from Arabic.

Hold up your algebraic formulae:

$X \times X = ?$
$XXV \times IV = ?$
$IX \times II = ?$

Ask the children, can they do these sums? Of course they can't. Explain that they are sums in Roman numerals:

I, II, III, IV, V, VI, VII, VIII, IX, X
= 1, 2, 3, 4, 5, 6, 7, 8, 9, 10

An I after V or X adds one to it; an I before V or X subtracts from it. There is no sign for 0 ('zero', 'cypher', both Arabic words). Confused?

Who gave us our numbers, including zero? Numbers that made it easier to add, subtract, multiply and divide? The Muslims.

$10 \times 10 = 20$
$25 \times 4 = 100$
$202 \div 2 = 101$

Now it makes sense.

Who founded the first universities? The Muslims. They were founded long before anyone had thought of our oldest universities, Oxford and Cambridge.

Meditation

Ask the children to close their eyes. Then say:

> *We thank God for those of the Islamic faith who brought good things, and the words for them, to our world: lemons, oranges and zeros.*

Some Muslim words, from the Qur'an:

> *Praise God. All things in heaven and on earth belong to him; praise him forever more. He is full of wisdom, and knows everything. He knows everything that goes into the earth, and everything that comes out of it . . . he is merciful and forgiving.*

Preparation: Nine candles.

It's time to get those candles out again. Or at least nine of them. There are actually eight nights of Hanukkah; the ninth candle is the 'servant' used to light the others. Light the first candle with the 'servant', and say:

One little candle
One little candle
One little candle burning bright.
Light the menorah
Light the menorah
Because it is Hanukkah tonight.

Light the second:

Two little candles
Two little candles
Two little candles burning bright
Light the menorah,
Light the menorah
Because it is Hanukkah tonight.

(Up, of course, to eight candles.)

The Jews have given us books about history and philosophy; they have given us stories; they have given us poetry. Many of these books are collected in the Old Testament of the Bible.

During Hanukkah, Jews say Psalm 117, which is a poem, and it goes like this. (The children should say the part in italics.)

O praise the Lord.
   All ye nations
   Praise him, all ye people.

O praise the Lord
   For his merciful kindness
   Is great towards us.

O praise the Lord
   And the truth of the Lord
   Endureth for ever.

O praise the Lord.

A story from the Jewish scriptures:

> *Once there was a young woman called Ruth whose husband had died. Her mother-in-law told her to go back to her home, but Ruth said these beautiful words:*
> *'Whither thou goest I will go; and where thou lodgest, I will lodge: thy people shall be my people, and thy God my God: where thou diest, I will die, and there I will be buried . . .'*

This is from the book of Ruth in the Bible, and one example of what the Jews have given to us.

A visit from a Jewish friend of the school to explain more about Hanukkah would be valuable. The children should be asked beforehand to think of questions they would like to ask him or her.

Here's a story for Christmas.

The story of St Nicholas:

> *There was a man who had been rich. He'd been rich once – but now he was poor. He had three daughters, and he was so poor that sometimes he couldn't feed them, or himself. He walked the streets looking for work. He'd have worked at anything, but he couldn't find anyone who'd pay him, not even to sweep the streets.*
>
> *Winter came and there was no coal to heat the house. The roof leaked, and rain and snow came into the rooms.*
>
> *The girls were at an age when they were thinking about marriage, but no one would marry anyone as poor as they were. In those days, young men married for wealth almost more than they married for love.*
>
> *The man despaired. He said to the girls: 'I must sell the three of you. I must sell the three of you as slaves. I must sell the three of you as slaves to some rich man. You will, at least, be warm in someone's house, and you will have enough to eat and drink.'*
>
> *Soon the whole town knew about the plan, and slave-traders came to see if the girls were worth buying. Were they strong enough? Would they live long lives?*
>
> *Others came to stare, because they were nosy and enjoyed looking at a rich man and his daughters who had become poor.*
>
> *Even the bishop heard about it. But he didn't go to stare at the poor man and his daughters. He decided to do something. He gathered together as many gold coins as he could, and he put them in three bags. Then he crept to the man's house at dead of night and climbed the walls. When he reached the roof, he dropped the first bag down the chimney.*
>
> *When the man and his daughters saw what was in the bag, and as they let the gold coins run through their fingers and tumble on to the floor, they couldn't believe their luck.*
>
> *The second night the bishop did the same, and the third. On the third night (have you noticed how there*

has to be three nights? Like three blind mice, and three bears, and three caskets: one of gold, one of silver, one of lead?) the man and his daughters were waiting for him, and they ran out of the house . . .

Only to see their bishop, robes hoicked up over his waist, so you could see his legs, running off up the street!

They ran after him till they were breathless, and they caught him, and thanked him. He swore them to secrecy. But soon, somehow, the whole town knew about the kindness of St Nicholas.

And St Nicholas is . . . FATHER CHRISTMAS!

You could also tell the story of Good King Wenceslas. And sing 'Good King Wenceslas'.

Spring

NEW YEAR RESOLUTIONS

Tell the children: 'I'm going to do better this year. Last year I . . .' Then name some naughty things, for example:

o Came into assembly without knowing what I was going to say.
o Ate too many Crunchie bars.
o Got cross with the cat.
o Hit my car on the bonnet when it wouldn't start.
o Told my sister I liked her dress, when I thought it was hideous.

This is year I am going to:

o Make sure I know what I am going to say when I come into assembly.
o Eat fewer Crunchie bars.
o Be kind to the cat when he's caught a baby bird.
o Keep the car in good condition so it doesn't let me down.
o Be honest about my sister's new clothes.

Ask the children: 'What about you and your resolutions? Have you made any?' Collect a few responses.

Then: 'How about this one: "This year I am going to understand what I am good at, and practise getting better and better at it."'

Announce to the children that, later this week, we are going to celebrate skills we have acquired outside school.

o 'Who has singing/dancing lessons?'
o 'Who is a good fisherman/woman?'
o 'Who goes to some non-contact martial arts group, such as Shotokan Karate?'

Tell them to let you know if they would like to demonstrate this skill in an assembly, or talk about it.

'I think we should make some resolutions as a school':

o To treat everybody in it with respect.
o To go home each day knowing something we didn't know when we came to school.
o To make something good every day (see Ideas 2 and 3).

This assembly is made up of children demonstrating largely out-of-school skills. Ask the children to prepare for the assembly in advance. And at least one teacher should be prepared to join in with something that they are good at.

In one school, a boy who was studying ballet dressed as a sailor and danced a hornpipe. In another, a girl demonstrated her karate moves. In the same school, a boy showed the rest of the school how to spin an off-break in a cricket match, with the headteacher the defeated batsman. 'And can you do a leg-break as well?' asked the head. He could.

Meditation

Let's think about something that we are good at, however small it seems to be:

o Collecting (Stamps? Dolls? Beer mats?)
o Cooking
o Cycling
o Golf
o Gymnastics
o Pottery
o Reading
o Writing

Leave a few moments silence. Then:

Lord of the Universe, you have given us skills. Help us to strengthen them, day by day. Amen.

Music: For this assembly, the children need to sing the song 'Morning has broken'.

Eleanor Farjeon, who wrote the words, was half-Jewish, half-gentile: her father was a Jew, her mother a Christian. Eleanor Farjeon became a Catholic.

The tune is an old Irish one: nobody knows who composed it. In the 1970s, it was a hit song by a singer called Cat Stevens. Later he converted to Islam, and became a devout follower of the prophet Mohammed ('Peace be upon him', as good Muslims say) and a believer in Allah. He changed his name to Youssef Islam.

The song is like a melting pot, with elements of Christianity, Judaism and Islam, as well as ancient Ireland.

We are like a melting pot. To this island have come: Celts, Romans, Saxons, Vikings, Normans, Jews, men and women from the Caribbean, Muslims, Sikhs, Hindus and many, many others. We sing this song, and celebrate the melting pot in our land.

Look at the words:

○ Who does 'his' refer to in the last line of the second verse?
○ Who can find two gardens in the Bible?

Here's one of the gardens:

And the Lord God planted a garden eastward in Eden; and there he put the man whom he had formed. And out of the ground made the Lord God to grow every tree that is pleasant to the sight, and good for food; the tree of life also in the midst of the garden, and the tree of knowledge of good and evil . . .

Discuss with the children: 'What would be in your perfect garden?'

Music: New Orleans jazz.

Martin Luther King was born on 15 January 1929. He lived at a time when, in many states in the USA, black people had to sit in a different part of the bus from white people. Black children went to different schools from white children. Black members of jazz bands had to use lifts in hotels normally used to carry laundry up and down floors, while only white people were allowed to use the passenger lifts. Black people weren't considered good enough to travel, learn, or live with white people. Then . . .

'I have a dream . . .', said Martin Luther King.

Ask the children to say this phrase.

Martin Luther King's dream was this: 'That one day this nation (The United States of America) will rise up and live out the true meaning of its creed: "all men are created equal" . . . That black children and white children will be able to join hands and walk together as brothers and sisters . . .'

That dream still isn't a reality in parts of the USA, or in our country. But we can make it a reality in our school.

'Do we all treat each other with respect? Have you got a dream? What's your dream?' Offer some of your own dreams, as trivial as you like:

○ I have a dream that [local football team] will gain promotion . . .
○ I have a dream that Year 6 will one day put their coats on the pegs, not on the floor . . .

But then go on to serious dreams:

○ That one day the world will be free of poverty
○ That one day the world will be free of violence.

53

Music: Ravi Shankar.

Tell the children the story of Mahatma Gandhi: he was born in India on 2 October 1869, and died on 30 January 1948. He believed, above everything else, in never hurting any man or woman, any boy or girl. Or any animal, for that matter.

Here are some of the things he said [it would be good to have these written out on placards and held up by children]:

○ 'You must be prepared to observe absolute non-violence. You must have no hatred in your hearts.'
○ 'The essence of true religious teaching is that one should serve and be friends with everyone.'
○ He believed in 'the brotherhood of all humankind'.
○ 'Although we have many bodies, we are but one soul.'
○ But he believed in fighting, and he won many battles.

Pause here. 'Absolute non-violence'? 'Believed in fighting'? 'Won many battles'. . . ?

Gandhi won many battles? Those words – non-violence, friends, brotherhood – don't sound like the words of a winner of battles. But Gandhi won battles without ever holding a gun or a bomb, or even raising a fist.

○ He won rights for the untouchables (Harijans). These were the lowest of the low in India.
○ He united Hindus and Muslims.
○ And he brought about the independence of India, making it free of British rule.

Gandhi has much to teach us in our school. Listen to those words, and say them after me:

> *We will have no hatred in our hearts.*
> *We will try to be friends with everyone.*
> *We belong to the brother- and sister-hood of all mankind.*

A motto for our school? One of those might work . . .

Music: Some romantic popular music.

Love, they say, is 'what makes the world go round'. Well, it is central to our existence. It is central to what makes us human. And, therefore, it is the centre of five assemblies. And it is central to this book.

Teach the children this charm for St Valentine's Eve: on going to bed, place your shoes in the form of a letter T, and say:

I place my shoes like a letter T
In hopes my true love I shall see
In his best clothes and his array
As he is now and every day.

There are many traditional rhymes about love. Here are some:

1

Matthew and Kimberley
Sitting in a tree
K.I.S.S.I.N.G.
First comes love,
Then comes marriage,
Then comes a baby
In a baby carriage.

2

I've lost my love
And I do not care.
I've lost my love
And I do not care.
I'll soon find another one
Better than the other one.
I've lost my love
And I do not care.

3

My boyfriend's name is Tony.
He comes from Macaroni
With a pimple on his toes
And two black toes

And this is how my story goes:

One day he brought me peaches,
One day he brought me pears,
One day he brought me fifty francs
And kissed me on the stairs.

One day I was out walking.
I saw my boyfriend talking
With a pretty little girl
With a pretty little curl
And this is what I did:
I threw back his peaches
And I threw back his pears
I threw back his fifty francs
And kicked him down the stairs.

And here's a modern poem:

LOVING GERTIE BEST

I love Hannah's hairstyle
And Danuella's dress.
I love Chloe's class – she is
A clear catwalk success –

But Gertie gets me giggling
And I love Gertie best.

I love Rita's writing,
I love Zara's art.
The music plays with Pol
Hammers in my heart –
I hear it from the north, the south,
The east and from the west –

But Gertie gets me giggling
And I love Gertie best.

I love Maggie's movement
When she's jiving in the gym.
I love Sabrina's soft good night
When disco lights are dim.
I love the way that Pippa passes
Every little test –

But Gertie gets me giggling
And I love Gertie best.

I love Eram's glossy hair,
I love Nasima's nose.
I love Farida's fingers
And her brightly painted toes.
I love Niamh and Norma
When I'm feeling sad and stressed –

But Gertie gets me giggling
And I love Gertie best.

FS

Tomorrow: more about love for St Valentine's Day.

Music: Some romantic popular music.

Preparation: A cup and a saucer.

Ask the children, 'What's today?' You could have some Valentine cards which you will jokingly (probably) tell the children you have been sent.

Ask the children: 'Who sends Valentine cards, and to whom?' They will offer 'my Mum to my Dad', 'my Dad to my step-mum', 'my sister to her boyfriend'.

Hold up the cup and saucer, and suggest: 'The cup to the saucer.'

The idea is to write a nonsense, whole-school poem that will, however nonsensical, have a resonance. If you have pairs of objects around, that will get them started. Then, they will offer:

o The book to the reader
o The shoe to the lace.

Then, widen this by suggesting that they think of objects outside the hall:

o The moon to the stars
o The sun to the sky
o The stone to the earth
o The tree to the leaf.

After a while suggest a line beginning 'God to –', or Humankind to –'.

Suggest that all the children write a few more lines in their classes and bring them to tomorrow's assembly. If they are written with fat, felt-tip pens on large pieces of sugar paper they will make a fine display in the hall.

Say: 'Here is a poem about love.' Then read 'Loving Gertie Best' (see Idea 38). Half the school should say the line 'But Gertie gets me giggling' and the other half the line 'And I love Gertie best'. You read the rest.

I got this marvellous idea from Mary Jane Drummond's book *Assessing Children's Learning* (2003, David Fulton).

Music: something Islamic.

Preparation: Bring in something you love in a relatively low sense, e.g. a CD, a book, a plant, a photograph album, a replica football shirt, a ring.

Read the poems round the hall (see Idea 39).

Collect children's responses about similar things that they love, such as

○ I love chips.
○ I love my cat.
○ I love my team.
○ I love my auntie.
○ I love my Mum.
○ I love my country.

Talk about how the word love means something different in each of those sentences. 'Love' is almost a completely different thing in the line about chips, compared to the line about Mum.

Here is an Islamic story.

There were two brothers. I don't know their names, but let's say they were Ruhon and Rahul [or two Islamic names from your school]. The older one, Ruhon, had a wife and three children (two girls, one boy). I don't know what they were called either, but let's call them [three names from your school].

The younger brother, Rahul, had no family. He only had himself to look after. Ruhon and Rahul ran a farm together. They shared everything: the work, the land, the harvest. When things went wrong (and they do, sometimes, for everybody) they shared these things. When things went right, they shared those things, too.

The younger brother was walking home from the farm one day. He stopped suddenly. 'Hang on a minute,' he said to himself. 'Hang on a minute. I'm on my own with no family to support. But my brother has a wife, a wife and three children – two girls, one boy. He should have more corn than me to feed his family.'

IDEA

40

LOVE

59

So, when it was night, he went to the barn where he stored his corn and carried six bags of it away, and put it in his brother's barn.

Later the same night, his brother was walking home from the farm. He stopped still, too, and he said to himself: 'Hang on a minute. Hang on a minute. I am a happy man, with my wife and three children (two girls, one boy). But my poor brother has no one. He should have more of the corn.' So he went to his store room and carried six bags to his brother's barn.

In the morning the brothers found that their barns had the same number of bags of corn as before. But neither brother told the other what had happened.

This happened again and again over many years. The children of the first brother (two girls, one boy) grew up and left home. But every year, each brother gave sacks to the other, in the dark of night.

'I love chips' was one of my sentences. But what those brothers were doing . . . that's love!

Ask the children: 'Who loved his brother the most?'

Tell the children: 'We started with the sort of love that pop songs talk about [quote some here]. That sort of love sometimes makes us giggle. We talked about Valentine cards, and who or what would send them to whom (or what). We talked about another kind of love, the love of brothers (or sisters, of course) for each other.'

Revise the story. Nothing to giggle about there . . . What was that love like?

○ It was practical: they did for each other what they believed was necessary.
○ It was secret: the brothers didn't boast about it.

St Paul wrote: 'Love suffers long, and is kind. It isn't envious, doesn't boast, behaves well, doesn't look after itself alone, doesn't think evil, and is glad for the truth.'

I Corinthians 13.4–7.

Please close your eyes. Now think of a friend. Think, as well, of someone who isn't your friend. Think of something kind about both of them. Think of something you might do today for them.

That is love.

LOVE: SUMMING IT UP

Music: Ravi Shankar.

Hiranyakasipu was a powerful king. He wanted to be more powerful, even, than the gods, so he told everyone in his country that, from now on, they were to worship him and not the gods. Because they were frightened, they did what the king told them.

Except one young man. Prahlada was the king's son and, in the morning, he opened the windows of his house and sang his hymns of praise to the god Vishnu.

The sound of Prahlada's singing woke his father. 'Who,' he shouted, 'is singing hymns of praise to the god Vishnu? No one may sing hymns of praise to anyone else – to anyone else *– they must sing them to ME!' His servant was quiet for a moment. Then he said: 'Prahlada, your son, is singing songs of praise to Vishnu.'*

The king ordered the boy to be brought before him. He was enraged. He lost his temper. He saw a red mist. He flew off the handle. He hit the roof. 'In this country,' he stormed, 'everyone worships me.'

'You are powerful, father,' said his son. 'But I worship the god Vishnu alone.'

The king threw his son into a dungeon and had him tortured. Then he left him on the streets to fend for himself. But Prahlada's faith was stronger than ever, and he went about the counryside praising Vishnu.

The king plotted against him, but he couldn't find a way of stopping his son. Yet his sister, Prahlada's aunt, Holika, could. She came up with a plan. She put on a fireproof cloak and tricked the young man into sitting with her on a pile of wood. Someone lit the wood and the flames went through Holika's cloak, and burned her to death. But Prahlada came out of the fire unhurt.

The king called his son to him. 'Worship me, and I will give you everything you want. Your god Vishnu is nowhere.'

'My god Vishnu is everywhere,' said the son.

'Even in this stone pillar?' cried the king, striking it with his sword. 'If you are in there, Vishnu, come and save Prahlada.'

And the pillar turned into a man-lion, the god
Vishnu himself. The king screamed in terror, and the
man-lion tore him to pieces.

And all the country turned with Prahlada to
worship the god Vishnu.

Meditation
A Hindu prayer.

O God,
We praise you
With our thoughts
As the sun praises you
In the morning.
Keep us in our care,
Forgive us our sins
And give us your love.

A visit from a Hindu friend of the school would be a
good follow-up here.

Daniel was the chief man in the land, under the king Darius. He did everything: arranged the king's dinner parties, organized his politics and ran the place. But he worshipped the one true god, the God of Israel.

The other top dogs were jealous of him. They would have liked to arrange the king's dinner parties, organize his politics and run the place. So they thought of a way to bring Daniel down.

They went to the king, and said 'O King, live forever'. That's what people had to say to kings in that place, in those times. 'We must make a new law: anyone who prays to a god who isn't you, O King Darius (live forever), should be thrown into a den of lions.'

They knew that Daniel would go on worshipping his God, the God of the Jews. 'And,' they said, 'this law, O King (live forever), like all the other laws, cannot be changed.'

The king agreed and the law was proclaimed throughout the land. But when Daniel heard about it, what did he do? He opened the windows in his house. He opened the doors, as wide as possible. He prayed three times a day to his God, the God of the Jews.

Daniel's enemies were hiding around the edges of his garden and heard him praying. Of course, they sneaked off to the king. They said: 'O King (live forever), have you not passed a law saying that anyone who prays to a god who isn't King Darius should be thrown into a den of lions?'

'That is true,' replied the king. 'And the law cannot be changed.'

'Well,' said Daniel's enemies. 'Well now, O King (live forever). This Daniel, this Daniel, this Daniel, who is a Jew, ignores you, and ... he prays to his God ... O King (live forever). Every day, every single day, three times, in his house.'

Then the king was very sorry about the law he'd passed. He was fond of Daniel, very fond. He thought and thought to find a way to save Daniel. But the top dogs said, 'O King (live forever), the laws you made cannot be changed.' And they threw Daniel into the den of lions.

The king went to his room and didn't eat, and didn't drink, and didn't sleep. In the morning he went to the den of lions and called out, 'Daniel, O Daniel, has the living God saved you?' And Daniel's voice came out of the cave, 'O King (live forever), my God has sent his angel, and the angel has shut the lions' mouths.'

So Daniel was taken out of the den, and no hurt was found on his body, because he believed in his God.

Daniel believed he had to be true to God. What should we always be true to?

○ Our families
○ Our beliefs
○ Our friendships.

Music: Use the usual calming music, if you feel music is necessary. But when the children are ready, play something martial and aggressive, for once, like 'Mars' from *The Planets* by Gustav Holst, or some heavy metal.

Ask the children what makes them angry. You will get responses like this:

o When my sister comes into my bedroom
o When my brother breaks my toys
o When my Mum won't let me stay up
o When my Dad says I can't watch television
o When I get bullied on the playground
o When the other team scores a winning goal in the last minute.

Tell them what makes you angry, starting with similar low-level things, such as:

o When the cat has been sick on the stairs
o When my son has left his underwear in the bathroom.

Read this extract from an unpublished story:

My head was as cold as a blanket of snow for a moment. Then it flamed up, and it was like a fire. It was full of sharpness, angles and triangles. It was full of reds and purples clashing with each other . . .

Ask the children: 'What is the inside of your head full of when you are angry?' Ask them to make angry faces, and to look at each other. Ask them to draw those angry faces when they get back to the classroom. Ask them to use big felt-tip pens and large sugar paper, and write sentences on the drawings about:

o What makes them angry
o What they feel in their brains when they are angry
o What colours they feel inside when they are angry.

Ask the children to bring the drawings in to tomorrow's assembly.

Read this kenning poem about anger:

Rage

is a ceaseless
pacing
round a suddenly too small house

the beat of a music I can't bear   brow-
beating my head   leaving no space
for thought or word or prayer

muzzles of guns
and thundering
orange flowers

a gang
in a side street
menacing

a meal thrown
at the pedal bin
nibbled by the forgotten cat

FS

Could some of the older children write some kennings
about what anger is?

Music: Play 'Mars' again.

Preparation: A rough and ready display of the anger pictures (Idea 44), probably unmounted, should have been put up in the hall.

Ask the children: 'What does that music make you feel?'

Go through the pictures that are big enough for the children to see. 'Let's look at those angry faces.' Read some of the sentences they have written. 'It isn't good, feeling angry. What can we do about it?' Take suggestions:

○ Counting from 1 to 10
○ Moving away from what's making us angry
○ Meditation.

Meditation

> *Help me, God, to understand that the angry me isn't the real me. Or the only me.*

There are many stories for children about anger. This tells us something about the high tendency for tantrums and bad temper during the time of our lives when we are growing up.

○ *Angry Arthur* by Hiawyn Oram
○ *Where the Wild Things Are* by Maurice Sendak
○ *Hannah's Good Mood Hunt* by Hiawyn Oram and Joanne Partis.

Tell the children that St Augustine was a Christian priest who lived from 354 to 430. He rose to the top, and became a bishop. After his death, he became a saint. When he was an old man, he wrote a book about all the things he had done that he was ashamed of. Here he is, telling us about an evening when he was a boy, and he went 'scrumping' (stealing fruit):

There was a pear tree near our vineyard. It was loaded with fruit that didn't look good, and didn't taste good. Late one night, a band of bad lads, including me, went down to the tree to shake the fruit down. We had stayed out longer than was allowed. This was our wicked habit. We took away an enormous amount of pears. We didn't eat them. We just threw them at the pigs. The real fun was in doing something that we weren't allowed to do, something that was forbidden.

Adapted by the author from The Penguin Book of Childhood, *ed. Michael Rosen.*

Tell the children a story about something you have done that was naughty. I tell them, for example, that sometimes, when I am alone in the house in the evening, I eat my dinner out of the saucepan to save on the washing up.

Ask them for confessions. Emphasize (this is very important) that you want mischief, rather than vileness. You don't want stories about torturing the cat or stealing from someone's purse. As triggers for their thoughts, offer keywords: 'holiday', 'Christmas', 'food', 'brother', 'sister' and the like.

They will tell stories about eating M&Ms from the kitchen cupboard and sharing them with the family dog; about losing their temper when they didn't get their way; about peeking at Christmas presents on Christmas Eve.

Make sure that some of the teachers have confessions to share. Talk about forgiveness. What does it mean?

Meditation

*Lord, I often do the things I shouldn't
And fail to do the things I should.
I'm sorry.
Help me to do the things I should
And not do the things I shouldn't.*

Adapted from St Paul.

CONFESSIONS

Music: Anything silly and trivial.

This is another story about Hannah and her Grandfather.

'Last night,' said Grandfather to Hannah when she came downstairs for breakfast, 'there was a storm in the kitchen. Lightning flashed from the teapot spout.'

'Really?' said Hannah, pouring milk on to her muesli.

'Last night,' said Grandfather to Hannah, 'there was a storm in the kitchen. Lightning flashed from the teapot spout, and thunder roared from the cooker.'

'Goodness,' said Hannah, putting a spoonful of cereal into her mouth.

'And last night,' said Grandfather to Hannah, 'there was a storm in the kitchen. Lightning flashed from the teapot spout, and thunder roared from the cooker . . . and rain gushed down from the ceiling.'

'Grandfather, are you joking?' said Hannah, fishing a piece of toast out of the toaster.

'No,' said Grandfather. 'I am not joking. And last night,' he continued, 'there was a storm in the kitchen. Lightning flashed from the teapot spout, and thunder roared from the cooker, and rain gushed down from the ceiling until there was a flood in the sink that splashed onto the floor.'

'Oh dear, Grandfather,' said Hannah, eating her toast in little mouthfuls – she was a very polite girl. 'What did you do?'

'Last night,' said Grandfather to Hannah, 'when there was a storm in the kitchen, and lightning flashed from the teapot spout, and thunder roared from the cooker, and rain gushed down from the ceiling, there was a flood in the sink that spread to the floor, I made a wish that it would all go away, and that the sun would shine in the middle of the night.'

'And what happened next?' said Hannah, sipping her chocolate, and looking at her Grandfather.

'Last night,' said Grandfather to Hannah, 'when there was a storm in the kitchen, and lightning flashed from the teapot spout, and thunder roared from the

cooker, and rain gushed down from the ceiling, and there was a flood in the sink that spread to the floor, and I made a wish that it would all go away and that the sun would shine in the middle of the night . . . the storm stopped, and the sun came out, and I sunbathed on the kitchen floor and . . .'

He paused.

'Yes?' said Hannah, wiping her mouth with her hand (she wasn't *that* polite).

'You came down for breakfast . . .'

'And?' said Hannah.

'And . . .' said Grandfather. 'I said: APRIL FOOL!'

FS

Music: A Shakespeare song is appropriate but not necessary.

Tell the children: 'Did you know that Shakespeare died on his birthday! He was born on 23 April 1564 and died on 23 April 1616. Here is something he wrote.'

A Midsummer Night's Dream

I'll follow you: I'll lead you about around,
Through bog, through bush, through brake, through
      briar;
Sometime a horse I'll be, sometime a hound,
A hog, a headless bear, sometime a fire,
And neigh, and bark, and grunt, and roar, and burn,
Like horse, hound, hog, bear, fire at every turn.

Act 1, Sc. 1, 87ff.

You should say these lines in a threatening way. You could say them phrase by phrase, with the children repeating each phrase after you. It is very effective if you say the words in a crescendo and a diminuendo: whispering the first line, slightly louder the second, louder still the third, shouting the fourth, then getting gradually quieter till the end, when you (and they) whisper again.

You could act these lines out, moving around the hall, lowering your head, lifting it up, keeping your eyes focused on what is immediately in front of you, occasionally 'terrifying' individual children . . .

Ask the children: 'Write a poem beginning "I'll follow you", but set, not in a forest, but in a school, or a supermarket, or in the solar system, or under the sea.' Point out how prepositions, like 'under', 'over', 'behind', etc. will help here. So will the word 'where', which will add interest: 'I'll follow you/through the automatic doors/where they slide open/without my asking them . . .'

As a footnote, point out that today is also St George's Day, and that very little is known about him. George never came to England. Ask the children to nominate an English man or woman as a better patron saint (they don't have to have been saints literally). For example, Winston Churchill, Florence Nightingale, Elizabeth I,

William Shakespeare. Nominations have to come with good reasons.

Or they could find out about two genuine candidates: St Alban, the first English martyr, and St Edmund, the Confessor. Get them researching using encyclopaedias and the Internet.

Music: A Shakespeare song is appropriate but not necessary.

Read the 'I'll follow you' poems written by the children for Idea 48. Divide the school into halves. Say this poem in this manner:

> *YOU: When that I was and a little tiny boy,*
> *FIRST GROUP: With hey, ho, the wind and the rain,*
> *YOU: A foolish thing was but a toy,*
> *SECOND GROUP: For the rain it raineth every day.*

. . . And so on for all the verses.

> *But when I came to man's estate,*
> *With hey, ho, the wind and the rain,*
> *'Gainst knaves and thieves men shut their gates,*
> *For the rain it raineth every day.*

> *But when I came, alas, to wive*
> *With hey, ho, the wind and the rain,*
> *By swaggering could I never thrive,*
> *For the rain it raineth every day.*

> *But when I came unto my beds,*
> *With hey, ho, the wind and the rain,*
> *With tosspots still had drunken heads,*
> *For the rain it raineth every day.*

> *A great while ago the world began,*
> *With hey, ho, the wind and the rain,*
> *But that's all one, our play is done*
> *For the rain it raineth every day.*

> *YOU: And we'll strive to please you every day.*

That song comes from *Twelfth Night*, by William Shakespeare. You could finish by reading a favourite passage of your own from the plays or the poems.

Preparation: Before this assembly, ask some children about their learning. What can they do or understand now that they couldn't a while ago? I did this in one school, and the children gave me these sentences:

○ I used to wear armbands in the swimming pool, but now I can swim without them.
○ I used to spell words wrong, but now I spell them right.
○ I used to be afraid of the dark, but now I am braver.
○ I used to scribble, but now I write.
○ I used to know my 2-times table, but now I know all my tables.

In the assembly hall, bring seven children out to the front, one from each year group. They should be typical in size for their ages. Show how children grow as each year goes by.

Tell the children: 'There are other ways of growing, apart from just in size.'

Ask one child from each year group to prepare a sentence answering the question: 'What have I learned recently?' Year 6 should be encouraged to compose complex sentences.

Read out the sentences that the children prepared, or ask the children to read the sentences aloud themselves. The teachers should prepare similar sentences.

Suggest to the children that learning never ends. Ask the children to write sentences like the one above. So we grow physically. And we also grow intellectually. How else do we grow? Emotionally, as we learn to think about other people's needs. When we were babies, we only thought about ourselves. Now, though, we think about what makes other people happy or sad.

Bring in your eight desert-island books. They should be varied: fiction, poetry, art books, history, science, old, new.

For example, they could be:

○ A novel you enjoyed as a child, and which you still enjoy: *Treasure Island*

○ A book you used to read to your baby son or daughter: *Peepo!*

○ An album of photographs taken on holiday

○ Something about science: a book about the solar system

○ Something geographical: a book of maps of places in Spain, or wherever you go on holiday

○ A big book of poetry: Charles Causley's *Collected Poems for Children*

○ *The Book of Common Prayer*

○ A good dictionary.

Read one of the books: *Peepo*, maybe; or a part of one.

Ask the teachers: what their desert-island books are. A teacher should read something from one of their books.

And ask the children: what their desert-island books are. Ask one child from each class to bring a book for another assembly.

Music: Saint-Saëns, 'Carnival of the Animals'.

This assembly is pure story, with no moral. It is aimed mostly at Key Stage 1.

THE HIGH MARMALADE CAT

The High Marmalade Cat likes to sit on roofs.
He likes to sit on the nesting box in our garden.
He thinks it's fun to sit on the roof of our house.
He even likes to sit on the roofs of houses where his friends live.

And – I'm afraid – he likes to sit on the roof of St Mary-le-Tower Church.

He loves, if he can, to sit among the flags on the Queen's roof. But he doesn't get up there very often.

And always, wherever he sits, people say, 'Look! There's the High Marmalade Cat sitting up there.'

When he feels like it he comes down, however high the roof, one paw after another, carefully, creeping down and down until he leaps the last bit – jump – and lands safe on the ground.

Then he wonders where his tea might be, and where he might get a cuddle.

Oh yes, the High Marmalade Cat likes to sit on roofs.

On Sunday last week, he climbed to a roof that was very high.

It wasn't the roof of the nesting box. It wasn't the roof of our house, not one of the roofs of the houses where his friends live. It wasn't the roof of St Mary-le-Tower Church. It wasn't the Queen's roof.

It was the highest roof of the airport. We could see the cat up there against the sky, looking round as the aeroplanes roared in and out.

I called my brother's rabbit, but she couldn't get the cat down.

I called my son Daniel's guinea-pig Eric, but he couldn't get the cat down.

I called the vicar's tortoise, but she couldn't get the cat down.

My brother's rabbit, Daniel's guinea pig Eric and the vicar's tortoise looked up at the High Marmalade Cat.

77

I called my big friendly dog, Jessie, but she couldn't get the cat down. I called my hamster, but she couldn't get the cat down.

I called my goldfish but – no, he couldn't get the cat down.

My brother's rabbit, Daniel's guinea pig Eric, the vicar's tortoise, my big friendly dog Jessie, my hamster and my goldfish all looked up at the High Marmalade Cat.

I called my favourite horse, but he couldn't get the cat down.

I called my uncle's sheep, but they couldn't get the cat down.

I called the lovely cow my father has in his field, but she couldn't get the cat down.

My brother's rabbit, Daniel's guinea pig Eric, the vicar's tortoise, my big friendly dog Jessie, my hamster, my goldfish, my favourite horse, my uncle's sheep and the lovely cow my father has in his field all looked up at the High Marmalade Cat.

I called for the Prime Minister's goat, but he couldn't get the cat down.

I called for the Queen's fiercest corgi, but she couldn't get the cat down.

Even I tried to get the cat down, but I couldn't. Of course.

My brother's rabbit, Daniel's guinea pig Eric, the vicar's tortoise, my big friendly dog Jessie, my hamster, my goldfish, my favourite horse, my uncle's sheep, the lovely cow my father has in his field, the Prime Minister's goat, the Queen's fiercest corgi and I all looked up at the High Marmalade Cat.

Then my son Daniel said, 'Look! Look!'

And the High Marmalade Cat came down.

He came down, one paw after another, carefully, creeping down and down over flat roofs, shiny roofs, sloped roofs, glass roofs, steep roofs until, at last, he leaped the last bit – and landed safely on the ground.

Then he came to Daniel for a cuddle, and back to our house for tea.

This is another animal assembly, but packed with morals.

Tell the children that in the Jain religion, which lives today in India, and in other places, there are two principles:

○ No human being should ever hurt another living creature.
○ Everything is eternal – it lasts forever.

Both these principles, put together, mean that everything in nature is holy, from the tiniest ant to the biggest elephant.

Leonardo da Vinci believed that animals were holy, too. (If possible, it would be a good idea to show the children some reproductions of Leonardo's work from books.) Here is a story about him.

He was walking in town one market day, taking time off from his work. He was an artist and a scientist. The air was full of the noises of people selling things and buying things: meat, vegetables and little nicknacks. He saw a man who was selling wild birds in cages.

Leonardo gazed at the birds for a long time, thinking. Then he took out his money and bought all the birds the man had to sell. The man couldn't believe his luck. He took the money and put it in his purse. Then Leonardo carried the cages to the top of a hill where there were trees, and carefully he opened the door of each cage, and set all the birds free.

He watched as they rose into the air, beating their wings for the first time in a long while.

William Blake wrote:

A Robin Redbreast in a Cage
Puts all Heaven in a Rage.
A dog starv'd at his master's gate
Predicts the ruin of the State,
A horse misus'd upon the road
Calls to Heaven for human blood.
Each outcry of the hunted hare
A fibre from the brain does tear,
A skylark wounded in the wing,
A cherubin does cease to sing.

From 'Auguries of Innocence 1'

IDEA

53

ANIMALS

Jesus tells us:

○ That God is interested in the fall of a sparrow.
○ That God knows so much about you that He has counted the number of hairs on your head.

Maybe the Jain religion is right: we should respect every single one of God's creatures.

Music: Something from a Bach mass ('O Sacred Head Sore Wounded', for example).

Here is the saddest part of the Easter story. It's from St Mark (14.22–the end).

Jesus ate his last supper with his friends. He said: 'Eat this bread. Drink this wine. They are my body and my blood.' And after dinner, they went out to the Mount of Olives. Jesus said to Peter, 'Tonight, before the cockerel crows twice, you will let me down.'

And Peter replied, 'I will never let you down.'

And they came to a place called Gethsemane, and Jesus asked most of his friends to wait. He went a little way off with Peter, James and John, and he told them that he was sad, sad to the point of death, and he began to pray:

'Father, take this cup away from me. Even so, let your will, not mine be done.'

Then he went to where Peter, James and John were waiting – and they were asleep.

'Peter,' said Jesus, shaking him. 'Could you not wait with me one hour? Watch, and say your prayers.'

And he went away again, and said the same prayers that he had said before. And when he came back, they were asleep again. And they didn't know what to say to him.

When he came back the third time, they were asleep yet again. And he said to them: 'Sleep. Take your rest. The hour is come. I am betrayed.'

Meditation

We all let a friend down at some time or another. And we have all been let down. Let's think, in the silence, of ways in which we can look after each other, especially at times when our friends are in trouble: sick, lonely, sad.

THE RUNAWAY SON

Here is one of Jesus' stories:

There was an old man who had two grown up sons. The younger one said to his father, 'Give me what I will have from you when you die.' So the father divided up all he had between the sons. The younger son sold everything and took the money, and left for a faraway country, and spent it all living a wild life. There were no pubs or nightclubs then in that part of the world, or in any other, but those places are where he would have spent his money if he had had any.

When he had spent it all, there was a famine in that country and he had no food. He got a job minding pigs on a farm. He would have been glad to fill his stomach with the pigswill. But no one gave him anything.

Then he came to his senses. 'My father's servants have more than they need to eat,' he said to himself. 'And I am starving to death. I will go to my father and say, "I am no longer right to be your son. I have sinned against both God and you. Please take me back as your servant."' So he started the long walk back to his father's house.

But when he was still far off, his father saw him – he'd been watching for him from a tall tower – and ran down the stairs of the tower and along the road. He ran up to his son, and he hugged him. And the young man said, 'I am no longer right to be your son. I have sinned against both God and you. Please take me back as your servant.'

But the old man called out, 'Give him a fine robe! A ring! Shoes for his tired feet!' And he ordered a feast. 'Because this son of mine was dead, and is now alive again. He was lost, and now he is found.' And the party began.

Meditation
God is like the best father, and loves us whatever we do.

'This son of mine was dead, and is now alive again.'

That was how yesterday's story ended (Idea 55). The boy had been dead to his father and was now alive to him. That is what Easter is all about. We see new life in the eggs when the chickens emerge; we see new life in the lambs in the field, tottering after their mothers. Most excitingly, we see new life in the birth of baby brothers and sisters.

But the story didn't end there. I hope that you remember that there were two brothers. The older brother had been working on the farm when his younger brother returned. He came into the house to find a party going on, with music, feasting and drinking.

He was angry. He said to his father: 'This isn't fair. I've worked faithfully for you, and you never gave me a party. Now this boy comes back, having wasted himself, his time and your money in a foreign land, and you throw him a party. It isn't fair.'

Ask the children: 'Have you ever said that?'

But the father said, 'This son of mine was dead, and is now alive again.'

And we see new life: in the eggs, in the lambs, in the blossoms growing all around our streets, in new babies being born, in the Christian story of Easter, and in the story of the young man who came back to his father, who still loved him.

NEW LIFE

It so happened that there were two men. They were walking, one dusty, hot afternoon, on a long road from a big city to a tiny village called Emmaus. They didn't want to be walking there. They'd expected something different.

They'd expected a walk in triumph, with a king leading them. This king would have led them and the rest of the people to freedom.

If you could have seen their eyes, you would have seen eyes full of misery. If you could have seen their shoulders, they would have been hunched. If you could have heard their voices, you would have heard words about a friend who had been executed.

Something had happened. Where was their king? Their king was dead. He had died on a cross.

And a stranger joined them on the road, and began to talk with them. He seemed to know everything about the history of their country.

They told him about their friend, the king who had been executed. 'We trusted in him, that he would save the country, that he would be a king. But the chief priests and rulers took him away and put him on a cross. And this was three days ago . . . You must have heard about him . . .'

And the stranger told them stories about the history of the country; and how the man who would save it had to suffer, and had to die.

And they came to the village where they were travelling, and the stranger began to walk on. But there was an inn. And they asked the stranger to stay with them. 'It is late,' they said, 'and the day is far gone. Eat some bread, and drink some wine.'

And they ate together. And the stranger broke the bread, and they saw who he was. He was the friend who had been killed. He was their king. And, at that instant, he disappeared from their sight.

And they said to each other, 'Did not our hearts burn within us as he broke that bread?'

Meditation

There is someone waiting, somewhere, who wants to be our friend. Help us to recognize him or her.

Music: For once, music with words. A song.

Play the music, and ask the children to listen to the words. Tell them that words and names are what make us human. Can your dog talk? Can your cat, or your hamster, write? Of course they can't. But you, all of you, can do both.

We use words everyday. I wonder how many words each of us uses in a single day. Tens of thousands, I should think.

Ask the children: 'Have you ever thought, some words are beautiful, and some are not so beautiful? I've made a list of my favourites.' Obviously, you will make your own list. Mine is: poem, path, Dad, cathedral, *cerveza* (Spanish for beer) and goat.

Having given the matter some thought, tell the children your six favourite words. Then ask them: 'Please close your eyes, and think of your own favourite words.'

It's important that the children have a minute to think about this: kneejerk reactions are useless. Also, teachers should be ready to offer their favourite words.

Next, challenge the children to:

○ Write a sentence containing all their favourite words.
○ Draw an illustration to depict their best one of all.

Then ask selected children to say their words to the whole school. Ask the children to listen hard so that they take notice of any word that comes up more than once or twice.

Here is a poem for this assembly:

FAVOURITE WORDS

Miss said, 'Please write down
your six favourite words'

and mine were 'path' and 'poem',
'jazz' and 'poetry',
'Daddy' and 'samosa'.

Jessica's were 'Jessica',
'purple' (her favourite colour),
'Jess', 'Amanda' (her middle name)
and 'bedroom' and 'me'.

Miss's were 'chocolate'
and 'chocolate' and 'chocolate'
and 'chocolate' and 'chocolate'
and, finally, 'chocolate'.

Craig said his were 'gun' and 'war',
'army-man' and 'CRASH!'
and 'tank' and 'submarine'.

And the new student teacher?
Hers were 'love' and 'peace'
'beach', 'sun', 'wine' and 'Jonathan'

and we all said
'Is that your boyfriend, Miss?'

You can tell a lot about people
from their favourite words.

FS

It is useful to have a dictionary of names for this assembly. Otherwise, see the list in the Appendix at the end of the book.

Tell the children: 'There is a very special word. What could it be? . . . It is your name. Whisper it to yourself.'

Then tell them the story of your name. Here is a model. It's about my name:

My name is Fred. When I was a little boy, I hated it, because none of the other boys were called Fred. I longed to be something I thought 'normal', like Michael, or Matthew or David.

I got my name because my Mum hadn't thought of what to call me. My Dad was still away fighting in a war, so he couldn't help. The nurses said: 'You'd better name him now, because if he dies without a name he won't go to heaven. Instead he will go to a place called Limbo, which isn't a pleasant place at all.'

So all my Mum could think of was her husband's name, Fred. I was called Freddie until he died. Then I became Fred.

I found out one day that my name is the word for 'peace' in Danish and Swedish. So it isn't such a bad name, after all.

When you've told the story of your name, and some of the teachers have too, ask the children, 'Who has a story about their name?'

In another school, six-year-old Christopher said: 'I don't like my name because it is too long. I would like to be called Gary, like my Dad.' And Shixin, who was ten, wrote this:

My name is Shixin. When it is written in Chinese, you can change it so that it means 'Die, heart'. My Mum was going to call me 'Shewonsing', but when someone said it, it sounded like 'She won't sing' so my Mum decided to change it . . .

Adam named the creatures. What would you call all the animals, now, if it were up to you? A dog could be 'Wagging-tailed Runner', a cat 'Sleeping Furball', etc.

ANOTHER SPECIAL WORD

Music: Anything peaceful, such as the adagio of
Schubert's String Quintet. The song 'Shalom aleichem'.

We have talked about favourite words (Idea 59). How
about 'peace'? Ask the children: 'Look at your hand. Go
on, choose one. Make a fist and look along your
knuckles. What do they look like?'

You are, of course, aiming to draw out similes here,
signalled, usually, by the word 'like', for example, 'like
mountains', 'like little hills', 'like boulders'.

'Look at your palm. What does it remind you of?
Road maps? Webs? What does your thumb look like? Or
your fingernails?'

Ask the children: 'What can you do with your hand?
Eat, drink, write, type, paint, draw, play the piano, wave
hello and goodbye, stroke the cat or the dog. And shake
hands.'

'Listen to these words: *Shalom, sholem, scholem, pax,
pace, paz, paix, irene, Frieden, fred*. They all mean "peace"
in, respectively, Hebrew, Yiddish, Arabic, Latin, Italian,
Spanish, French, Greek, German and Danish. Do you
know the word for "peace" in any other languages? Turn
to a friend, shake hands and say "*Shalom*".'

The song to sing for this assembly is 'Shalom
aleichem'.

Tell the children: 'Of course, in some cultures, you
can pray with your hands. Put them together now. Make
your prayer a wish. Then direct it to God.'

Summer

Music: There is a song by a Pharoah. It is 'Hymn to the Sun' from Philip Glass's opera *Akenhaten*. It is not absolutely necessary, but would add atmosphere.

Tell the children:

> *There was a Pharoah who loved the sun. He loved it so much that he threw away all the Egyptian gods – Isis and Osiris and the rest – and worshipped only the sun, the disc in the heavens that gave heat and light and life to everything. The Pharoah's name was Akhenaten, and this is a song he wrote to the sun.*

Ask the children to say the repeated line, here printed in italics:

TO THE SUN

> *You created the earth*

When you were far away
Men, cattle, all flocks
Everything on earth moving with legs,
Creeping, stalking, striding,
Or flying and gliding above with wings.

> *You created the earth*

Foreign countries
And the land of Egypt:
You placed every man in his place
And you provide his food.

> *You created the earth*

You are the Creator or Months
And the Maker of days.
You are the Counter of Hours!

> *You created the earth*

You shine on the eastern horizon
And fill the whole earth with your beauty
And while you are far away
Your beams shine in every face.

> *You created the earth*

When you shine
Creatures live.
When you set
They die.
You yourself
Are lifetime.
The creatures live in you.

You created the earth

Living disc,
Lord of all that was created
And which exists!
Your beams have brightened
The whole earth.

You created the earth

Adapted by FS from traditional sources

Some people use the term 'sun-worshipper', even today.
Ask the children: 'What do they mean?'

And ask the children: 'What would happen to the
earth and all its creatures if the sun died tomorrow?'

No wonder different peoples have worshipped the
sun! Ask the children to research sun-worshipping
peoples.

Music: Anything American, from 'The Star-spangled
Banner' through to jazz or modern pop. Or Aaron
Copland's 'Billy the Kid', 'Appalachian Spring' or
'Rodeo': quintessentially American pieces.

Tell the children: 'Every year, on the 4th of July, the
people of the United States of America celebrate their
breaking away from British rule, in 1776.

'But the men and women who had sailed to America
in 1620 were not the first Americans. The native
Americans, whom people used to call 'Red Indians', tell
many stories. Here is one:'

SCARFACE

Tall Tree was a sad Apache brave.

*I'll tell you why he was sad: two reasons. One, his
mother and father had died saving him from a wild
bear when he was a baby. That would make anyone
sad.*

*And, two, Tall Tree himself had a scar on his face.
The bear had given him that. This scar stretched from
above his ear to his chin.*

The other braves called him Scarface.

*Tall Tree's chief, Fat Buffalo, had a daughter. All
the young men admired her. But the young man who
loved her best was . . . can you guess? . . . Yes, it was
Tall Tree.*

*Happy Flower was the name of the girl, and she
loved Tall Tree. She knew he was kind and honest, and
would never cheat anyone, or take anything that did
not belong to him.*

*But Happy Flower was under a spell from the sun
god, a spell that meant she could marry no one.*

*Tall Tree decided to travel over the Blue Mountains
to where the sun god lived, and ask him to lift the spell
from Happy Flower and to take away the scar from his
face.*

*He travelled for many months, until he came close
to the sun god's palace.*

*He found a bow and arrows on the ground,
beautiful and strong, but he left them where they were,
because they belonged to someone else.*

Then he met a young man. The son of the sun god! He was called Quick of Foot, and he told Tall Tree that he had lost his bow and arrows. Of course, Tall Tree showed him where they were.

They became friends, and often went hunting together. Sometimes they went hunting where they had been told not to go, among evil spirits.

These spirits were birds, with beaks wide and talons sharp. And they flew like darts, like arrows, at the young men. Quick of Foot collapsed on the ground, exhausted and wounded. He'd been stabbed by the beaks, and torn by the talons. He was about to die. Tall Tree fought on alone, until he had used his last arrow, and killed the last of the evil spirits.

He carried Quick of Foot home to his father.

The sun god was, of course, grateful to Tall Tree for saving his son and offered him anything he would like.

And he lost his scar and his ugly nickname, and the sun god said he could marry Happy Flower.

Music (by no means necessary): The theme music from *Chariots of Fire* by Vangelis.

In Olympics year, which comes around every four, get some children to prepare for this assembly by using the *Guinness Book of Records* or the Internet to find out records for the:

o Long jump
o High jump
o 100 metres
o 1,000 metres
o 5,000 metres
o Marathon.

Then, measure the long jump record on the floor in children-lengths. Ask a teacher to demonstrate the triple jump. Clap your hands for the beginning of the 100 metres, and again when the record time has elapsed.

Ask the children: 'What is athletics for?' Collect answers:

o To keep us fit.
o To experience the thrill of winning.
o To experience the beauty of the human body at its best, even if it is only Mr ___ or Ms ___ doing the triple jump . . . ('Show us again, Mr ___ or Ms ___ . . .').

A teacher could demonstrate other sports: a defensive shot in cricket, for example.

Challenge the children to run their own 100 metres races in the playground.

Music (again by no means necessary): 'Food, Glorious Food' from Lionel Bart's *Oliver*.

Collect together various foods (packaging will do for many, though not all):

○ Tinned vegetables
○ Crisps
○ Salad – tomatoes, lettuce, radishes, spring onions
○ Fresh fruit – apples, pears, grapes, bananas
○ Fresh vegetables (include at least one vegetable that the children might not recognize: a courgette, for example)
○ Two kinds of cereal: one sugar-filled and the other fibrous
○ Sweets
○ Bread: white and brown
○ Fizzy drinks
○ Fruit juices and smoothies
○ Pizzas
○ Pies
○ Meat
○ Fish.

Ask the children to arrange them in three groups:

○ Healthy – must eat every day
○ Healthy – but eat only sometimes, and in moderation
○ Unhealthy – eat only as a treat.

Discuss using questions like 'What makes this food healthy or unhealthy?'.

When the assembly is over, make it clear that the food will not be wasted. Indeed, some of it will be eaten by the children. Especially the healthy stuff.

IDEA 65

EXERCISE

There is, in every school, at least one child who knows more than everyone else about gymanstics, martial arts, ballet, yoga, or some other specialized area of the physical arts not always taught in school. Ask this child to demonstrate their skill. Then ask the children: 'What could each of you do to make yourself fitter?'

Breathing is one thing. Do a deep breath with the children. Slowly rise on your toes, while simultaneously raising your arms from the side of your thighs till your fingers meet above your head. In the meantime, draw in a long breath. Typically, the children will forget to stretch their feet and fingers. Remind them that they should. Demonstrate.

This will relax the children. When they have sat down, ask them to close their eyes and to imagine themselves as they exercise, and to make drawings or paintings of themselves exercising.

Meditation

My body is my own, and it is my God's. It is the temple of the Holy Spirit. How can I best look after it? What should I eat and drink? What should I do with it?

Sometimes one can base an assembly on a familiar object, but placed in an unfamiliar position, or in an unfamiliar setting.

You can, for example, get a remarkable amount of learning from a bicycle that has been set upside down in the hall as the children come into assembly. Upside down, because that makes the bike less familiar, and therefore easier to observe accurately. The hall, of course, has provided the unfamiliar setting.

Tell the children: 'We depend on ordinary things – the cooker that makes raw food edible, the television that gives us images, the Playstation that gives us pleasure, the book that thrills us.' Collect from the children some suggestions of other ordinary things on which we depend. This assembly is about something very ordinary: a bicycle. Take the children through the possible learning here:

○ **Science** All science begins with observation. Ask the children to watch as you turn the pedals. Ask: 'Why do the wheels turn faster than the pedals?" Discuss gears. Ask the children to close their eyes and listen as the wheels turn.
○ **Mathematics** Ask the children to identify all the shapes in the bicycle.
○ **History** Ask the children to research, in encyclo-paedias or on the Internet, the history of the bicycle.

Can the children think of other ordinary things worth looking at and listening to? Or researching? Can you bring in something ordinary?

Ask the children to draw something ordinary – a bicycle is only one example – and bring the drawings into tomorrow's assembly.

There's a chance here for a lesson about safety – good riding, helmets and the rest.

NATURAL ORDINARY THINGS

Music: An ideal hymn here is 'Daisies are our silver'.

Preparation: Have on display drawings and objects that children have brought in (see Idea 66).

Say to the children: 'Now let's think of ordinary things that aren't made by humans: things made by nature, or by God.'

Display some things that are routinely ignored, such as a leaf, a stone, a blade of grass, a twig. William Blake said that we should see 'a World in a Grain of Sand'. The next line in this poem tells us we should also see 'Heaven in a Wild Flower' ('Auguries of Innocence' 1).

Collect metaphors for the various objects: The veins on a leaf are like . . . The twig remnds me of . . . The stone resembles . . . The blades of grass are shaped like . . .

Ask the children to make some closely observed drawings of natural objects.

Music: Anything swashbuckling.

Sometimes men and women have names that don't suit them. This is the story of John Little, who was more than two metres high. That's this high [demonstrate on the wall].

This story starts with an old English hero, Robin Hood.

He'd been hunting deer with his men, and they'd found nothing. Robin was sad, and he told his men that he was going off on his own. He probably wanted to have a think by himself. All of us feel like that sometimes.

'And,' he said, 'if I get into any danger, I'll blow my horn, and you must come and help me.'

He walked off, carrying nothing but his bow and his quiver full of arrows, and came to a river. There was a bridge. A very narrow bridge. It was made of rough planks, and had banisters of rope. Robin was walking across it . . . [this should be demonstrated on a 'pretend' rope] *. . . when he met a huge man in the middle.*

'You had better go back,' Robin said to the huge man, 'and let me get to the other side.'

But the huge man said, 'No, you had better go back, my friend, and let me *get to the other side.'*

And neither man would budge.

So Robin took his bow and fitted an arrow, and aimed at the big man.

'Oh!' exclaimed the big man. 'You would shoot arrows at me when I am only a metre from you, and I have only a stave, would you?'

'Fair enough,' said Robin, putting his bow and arrows away. He went into the nearby wood and found a stick. 'We'll do it this way, you ruffian. Whoever knocks the other into the stream will be the winner.'

And they began to beat each other about the head and body. The big man used his stave, Robin his stick.

Robin got such a crack on his head that blood spurted from it. He was so furious that he swung his stick wildly, and the swing took him head first into the river.

The big man laughed.

'Where are you now, man?' he cried.

'You have won. You are the better fighter,' said Robin. And, blood pouring from his head, he hauled himself out of the stream, took out his horn and blew it.

Immediately, 50 men in green appeared from out of the wood.

'Are you all right, master? Shall we knock this giant into the river for you?'

'No,' said Robin. 'He is brave and strong, and will be a part of our gang. And he will wear green, like us.'

But they changed his name. The giant had always been John Little. But now he was Little John.

Meditation

The person you feel like fighting with could become a friend.

Music: Something very quiet and meditative.

This may sound too heavy for primary schoolchildren, but I have done this exercise with six-year-olds and upwards and it always works. It makes for a thoughtful assembly.

Write on the overhead projector, a whiteboard or a flip-chart the word 'Philo'. Explain that it is ancient Greek for 'Friend'. Now write 'Sophy'. Explain that it means 'Knowledge' or 'Wisdom'.

Put the two words together: 'Philosophy'. This means 'friend of knowledge' or 'wisdom'.

Tell the children that today we are going to be philosophers for ten minutes, and ask them: 'Can you think of a question that you'd love to know the answer to, but you know you never will?' Explain that it must not be a question that they could look up in a book. Also, you don't want practical questions, like 'How does a car work?'

Suggest words to begin the kind of question you want: Why? When? Will? Can? Do? Does?

Ask the children to close their eyes and cover them with their hands for about a minute, while they think of their questions. Then collect what they suggest. You will get questions like:

- Will there be another war?
- Why did my Granddad die?
- How can I tell if a man is evil or not?

Then repeat the exercise. This time suggest words that they might use in their questions, such as: peace, love, hate, death, God, devil. And collect more questions. Over the years I have been offered:

- Does God believe in me?
- Will my Granddad go to heaven even if he wasn't a Christian?
- Do cats dream?
- Why do adults have power over children and not the other way around?
- How does gravity hold you down?
- How did God get made?
- How does the sea suck you away?

Ask the children to write their questions down on large pieces of paper when they get back to class, and to bring them to the hall during the day to be pinned up on the walls.

Music: Meditative music.

The next day, walk around the hall, reading out the philosophical questions that the children have placed there (Idea 69).

Say a prayer for wisdom:

Help me, God, to search for the truth.
Help me to know that I may find it where I least
    expect it:
In my friend's eyes,
In my family's love,
In the work I plan to do today.
Amen.

A great philosophical question is 'What is the good life?' Collect answers. Prompt words might be: health, wealth, money, happiness . . .

DON'T STOP BEING A PHILOSOPHER

THE LOVE OF MONEY

Ask the children: 'How would you like it if everything you touched turned instantly to gold?' Collect some responses. Then tell this story, adapted from the Roman poet Ovid:

A king called Midas had done a favour to his god, Bacchus. The god was grateful, and promised Midas that, as a reward, he could have whatever he liked.

Ask the children: 'If the god had said this to you, what would you have asked for?' Collect some responses.

A dream had been floating in Midas's head for years. It wasn't for peace, or love, or his family's or his country's happiness. It was a dangerous dream. Now, when he heard the god's promise, his eyes lit up. He could make his dream come true. 'Make it, Bacchus, so that everything I touch turns into the finest gold.'

The god was worried by Midas's greed. But he had promised, and so he granted the wish. 'Everything you touch, Midas,' he said, 'will turn to gold.'

Midas went home to his garden. Nervously, he walked down the stairs and approached the first tree, an oak. He reached out his hand, touched it – and suddenly the whole tree was turned into the best gold. He picked up a rock, and the rock was gold too. The king felt glad in his heart at the prospect of so much gold, so much happiness. The grass, the corn . . .

Soon the whole garden gleamed in the bright sunshine. It was a garden made of gold.

But . . . the corn! When the corn turned to gold, Midas's brow furrowed. He became thoughtful. He had been looking forward to eating it.

And the apple, too, from his best apple tree. This tree gave him perfect fruit every year. Now, however, it gave him something perfect – but it was perfect gold, and, of course, he couldn't eat it.

As he walked back into the palace, the pillars and walls turned to gold as he touched them. The water he washed his hands with was suddenly liquid gold.

At dinner time, of course, he could not eat. The instant he touched them, the meat, the vegetables and the bread, all became heavy with gold.

What do you think happened? Of course, he began to starve. Then he came to his senses, rather like the runaway son I told you about (Ideas 55 and 56), and called out to the god, 'I have been a greedy fool. Please take this gift away from me.'

And the god pitied Midas. 'Go,' he said, 'and wash yourself in the river.'

And when Midas immersed himself in the water, everything returned to normal, and Midas could never bear the look of gold anywhere near him ever again.

St Paul wrote: 'The love of money is the root of all evil.'

In what ways can the love of money cause evil? Examples are:

○ War
○ Theft.

Music: A CD by Billie Holiday.

Begin with a track and ask the children to identify the instruments. They will pick out trumpet, drums and others. Pick out for them the tenor and alto sax. 'But', you say, 'there is a more important instrument here, and it is the voice that belongs to Billie Holiday.'

Many years ago, African Americans were used as slaves by the white people of the United States of America. They were made to work for no wages. When slavery was abolished by President Abraham Lincoln, discrimination continued, and even in the 1960s, in many states, white children went to different schools from black children, and black travellers had to sit in different parts of buses from white people.

In the southern states, an organization called the Ku Klux Klan sometimes murdered black men. This was called lynching. Many white men would surround and kill a single black man.

Read the children the words of Billie Holliday, here adapted. She was the only black person in an all-white band:

> *I was billed next to Artie* [Shaw, the leader], *but was never allowed to enter the dining room, as other members of the band could. I had to enter and leave the hotel through the kitchen. I had to stay in a little dark room all evening, until I came out to sing my songs. Someone told Artie that I shouldn't be allowed to use the passenger lift, so after that I had to use the goods lift. When you're on stage you're great, when you're off stage you're nothing.*

End with 'Strange Fruit', a song about a lynching in the deep south.

Tell the children: 'Black Americans gave the world one of the greatest gifts of the twentieth century: jazz music. Here are some of their names: Louis Armstrong, Bessie Smith, Duke Ellington, Jelly Roll Morton, Sidney Bechet . . . and Billie Holiday.'

Ask the children: 'Have you ever felt anyone was unfair to you because of something over which you had no control?' Collect some responses.

Tell the children: 'You are all citizens, and so am I, and so are all the adults in our school. A citizen is a man or a woman who lives in a place. We are all citizens of at least four places (maybe five). Here are the first four:

○ The school
○ The town, village, or city we live in
○ The land we live in
○ The world.'

Being a citizen brings us:

○ **Rights** To be free of bullying and racism and any kind of prejudice.
○ **Duties and responsibilities** Such as being on the school council; looking after the environment: clearing up litter; caring for everything we share; encouraging democracy.

The authors of the Declaration of Independence (USA, 4 July 1776) wrote this:

We hold these truths to be self-evident, that all men are created equal, and that they are endowed by their Creator with certain unalienable Rights, that among these are Life, Liberty and the pursuit of Happiness.

I mentioned at the beginning that there might be a fifth place where we are citizens. Some people believe we are citizens of another place: the Kingdom of Heaven. Or you could call it (as Philip Pullman does in his trilogy of novels *His Dark Materials*) "the Republic of Heaven".'

READING THE NEWSPAPER

Take in today's paper, and read some stories:

o A sad one, about a family, perhaps
o A heart-warming one
o A funny one
o One about war
o A sports story (about the local football team, perhaps).

Discuss the stories with the children. 'Is there one that makes you want to pray?' Ask for responses. 'What would you say in a prayer about this story?'

Ask some children to work the prayers up by writing them down in their classrooms. During the day, they should make a prayer wall with an LSA's help.

Meditation
The world is both a terrible and a wonderful place, full of good and bad. Help us to stand up to the terrible, and to rejoice in the wonderful.

Music: Ask the pianist (assuming you have one) to play some beautiful, calming music.

Then say to the pianist: 'Don't bother. A piano can only make ugly sounds.'

The pianist, or someone else, could attack something you are well-known for loving: ballet, Morris dancing, karate, bird-watching.

Then calm things down, and say, 'Here's an ugly word for an ugly thing: BIGOTRY.' This word should be written on a card, large and ugly. Hold it up or display it on the wall.

Tell the children: 'Bigotry means sticking to a point of view, even though the evidence tells you that you are wrong. For example, "A piano can only make ugly sounds."' Here the pianist makes beautiful sounds on the piano, again.

'Or "All boys have bad manners."' Here some boy provides an example of good manners. 'Or "Girls are no good at football."' Here a girl expertly passes a ball across the hall, or heads it, or catches a high ball like a goalkeeper.

But there are bigger things to be bigoted about than the piano, or football or manners. Here are some:

- All older people are out-of-date and slow.
- All young people are silly.
- The bigotry displayed to Billie Holiday (in Idea 72) was of the worst kind, because it attacked her humanity: what she saw as her race, what was her background, her colour. What and who she was.

'In our school it is not allowed to be bigoted. Whatever happens in the rest of the world, this is true of our school':

Now is the time to make justice a reality for all of God's children.

'Martin Luther King said these words. He fought for the rights of every human being to be treated "justly". Can you think of another word for "just"?

Spend some time today thinking about how we might help to make our school a place where justice is a reality for all of us.'

Here's another story about Hannah and her Grandfather.

Grandfather was sitting with Hannah in the living room of her parents' house. He was in a chair and Hannah was on the settee. Suddenly, he looked up from his newspaper and said:

'You are lucky living in a house, Hannah.'

'What do you mean?' said Hannah. 'Everyone lives in a house.'

'Oh no, they don't,' said Grandfather. 'Some people live in flats, some live in tents, some live in caravans. Some have nowhere to live, except the streets.

'Some live on cold mountains, when their houses have been destroyed. Perhaps there has been a war, or an earthquake, and the people have had to run away from their homes.'

He paused for a moment. Hannah waited.

'When I was a baby, I had nowhere to live.'

Hannah was shocked. 'What happened to you?' she asked.

'Well,' said Grandfather. 'My Mum had nowhere to go when she came to London. Nowhere at all. She had almost no money.

'She found a house. It made everybody welcome. Inside there was food and comfort, and other people who had no homes.

'Because she was a nurse, trained in another country, they let her stay if she helped to look after the other homeless people.

'So that is how I began to grow up as a Barnardo's boy.'

Hannah looked at her Grandfather. She was trying to think of him without a house to call his own. She got up from the settee, and gave him a hug.

FS

Dr Barnardo was born in Dublin on the 4 July 1845. He was shocked to see children on the streets with nowhere to go, so he set up homes for them.

Everyone was welcome, he said. And he made sure that the homes provided the best care. In 1870, he founded his first home for boys, in 1876 his first home for girls.

Meditation

Everyday we can see homeless people on the streets of our town. What should we do for them?' Collect some suggestions.

Jesus said: 'The foxes have holes, and the birds of the air have nests; but the Son of man hath nowhere to lay his head.' (St Matthew)

So Jesus ('The Son of man') was a homeless person.

RIDDLES

Say to the children: 'Listen to this riddle and try to work out what I am describing. Please don't put your hands up till I've got to the last word, which is "dog".' The idea is to keep them listening and thinking, rather than competing, which is what they are doing when they put their hands up:

> *I am one of an endless family,*
> *My brothers and sisters*
> *Never far behind.*
> *I crash and swirl, grind pebbles, growl,*
> *And gnaw the bones of the land*
> *Like a great wet dog.*

> *John Cotton*

Say it again, while the children close their eyes and think about the riddle.

Here is another:

> *Within white seamless walls*
> *I store my treasure,*
> *A gold that nourishes.*
> *Search as you will*
> *You will find no opening in me.*
> *Once shattered I am not for mending.*

> *John Cotton*

And another:

> *Among all things wonderful –*
> *I saw this, the most wonderful of all –*
> *water becoming bone.*

> *Anglo-Saxon, trans. Emily Roeves*

And another:

> *I am an emerald umbrella*
> *opening towards the clouds.*
> *I leave clothes on the floor*
> *before revealing*
> *my new spring collection.*

My less fashion-conscious relatives
wear the outfit,
year in, year out.

Written by a group of Durham teachers

And two more:

I run steadily shaping myself differently wherever I go
over sharp and smooth never scratching myself
because I don't have skin.

I babble even though I cannot speak, and gurgle
even though I have no mouth.
I follow my path wherever I go. Making
images of wherever I may be.

Rosie, 10

Riddles make us think. They make us think about both things and words.

Produce some homely objects, such as an apple, a light bulb, a CD, a mirror. Ask the children to spend some time thinking of a riddle for one of them. It should begin 'I' or 'My', because the object speaks the riddle.

Here's a final riddle:

I have a hundred faces,
    Two hundred eyes.
Some parts of me are happy,
    Some are full of sighs.

Parts of me are topped with gold,
    Parts with brown.
I am a strange many-headed creature
    In a strange town.

FS

The answer, of course, is your school. (Adjust the numbers appropriately.)

This assembly contains ten poems. None of them is more than ten lines long. Most are even shorter. Write the poems on cards, and say them. And then ask the children to choose one and memorize it.

A LAKE

A lake
Is a river curled and asleep like a snake.

T. L. Beddoes

A poem in one-and-a bit lines? There's a thought. Poems can be very short. Here are five poems, each in four lines. The first two are by Christina Rossetti.

What is heavy? Sea, sand and sorrow.
What are brief? Today and tomorrow.
What are frail? Spring blossoms and youth.
What are deep? The ocean and truth.

My baby has a mottled fist,
My baby has a neck in creases;
My baby kisses and is kissed,
For he's the very thing for kisses.

Here are two by modern poets:

WAITING FOR A LETTER FROM THE ONE YOU LOVE

Nothing in the mailbox,
Nothing through the door,
Only a rusting spider
That was there before.

John Cotton

WAITING FOR AN EMAIL FROM THE ONE YOU LOVE

Open Outlook Express.
Has anyone written to my address?
What a depressing sight.
This lot were all there last night.

FS

And here's one by Shakespeare:

Jog on, jog on, the footpath way,
And merrily hent the stile-a:
A merry heart goes all the way,
Your sad tires in a mile-a.

The Winter's Tale

Here's a very old poem. It's so old, no one knows who wrote it:

THREE THINGS ARE TOO WONDERFUL FOR ME

Three things are too wonderful for me;
Four I do not understand;
The way of an eagle in the sky,
The way of a snake on the rock,
The way of a ship on the high seas;
And the way of a man with a maid.

Proverbs 30.18–19

And here's a little poem written by a ten-year-old boy:

A TREE CLIMBER TO HIS MOTHER

You are
the safety net
under every branch
I stand on.

Geraint, 10 years old

This poem dates from ancient history:

A BATTERSEA DOG

We got him in Battersea twelve years since.
We loved his bark and the symmetrical prints
 Of his paws
 On shiny floors
But last week the dark chose him, or he chose the dark.
I listen at night, and I cannot hear him bark.

After the Greek of Tymnes 2nd century BC.
Version by Emily Roeves and FS

And here is the shortest poem ever written, something that the headteacher said when she saw me running out of school on 21 July last year to buy an ice cream from Pelozzi's van:

Hey!

FS

Ask the children, 'What is the point of poetry?'. To make the writer and the reader:

o look
o listen
o think, and . . .
o derive pleasure.

Can you write a very short poem?

Here's another story about Hannah and her Grandfather.

Grandfather and Hannah had both grown up in towns. They loved the noise of traffic: cars, buses, ambulance sirens. Noise and bustle were part of their lives.

But now they were staying in the countryside. Hannah's parents had booked a two-week holiday in a little cottage. They were 'miles', as they kept saying, 'from anywhere'. The cottage had no phone.

And Grandfather and Hannah were loving that, too. It was quiet: from her bedroom in the morning, all Hannah could hear was birdsong. She ate her breakfast and listened to the quiet.

And, at night, she could see the stars.

One afternoon, Grandfather said, 'I'll take you out to a dance tonight. We'll go to a barn dance at the church hall in the village, and Mum and Dad can have an evening doing what they want.'

All evening, Grandfather and Hannah danced. Hannah danced with the children from the local school, and made friends with some of them. Grandfather danced with the vicar's wife.

It was dark when they began their walk home. Both of them were startled by how navy blue everything was. The sky was clear, and they could see the stars. Hannah felt she could learn to know them, so clear they were. Grandfather pointed out the Hunter and the Plough.

[You could show the children diagrams of these constellations, and ask them to look for them on a clear night before bedtime.]

The moon was full, and it cast a ghostly light on everything. A cloud drifted over the moon, and the night became darker. But Hannah didn't mind as she marched along the road holding her Grandfather's hand.

They turned off the road, and on to the path to the cottage. The moon disappeared. Now it was very dark indeed, and Hannah felt nervous. They continued walking. They climbed a stile. The crossed a cattle grid. The path on the other side went across a field.

Then Hannah stopped. Ahead of them was a
black, smooth shape. It seemed to make a sound like a
ghost escaping, a great sigh, deep and terrible.
Grandfather stopped too.

'What is it?' whispered Hannah.

'I don't know,' said Grandfather.

Hand in hand, they crept closer to the shape, which
seemed to be in their way.

It made its great sigh again. They found they could
walk past it, but they would be very close to it.

Grandfather laughed, suddenly. Very quietly.

'What is it?' Hannah asked, still scared.

'It is, my little treasure,' said Grandfather, 'it is –
a cow.'

In the morning, Grandfather said to Mum and
Dad, 'Last night we were frightened of a cow!'

'But,' said Hannah, 'we'll never be frightened of
one again, will we, Grandfather?'

'No,' said Grandfather.

FS

If your children are country children, ask them what is
frightening about towns. And if your children are town
children, ask them what is frightening about the country.

In a moment of quiet, ask the children to think of
something that frightens them – and to think about what
they are going to do about it.

Ask a brave child to come out and sit next to you. He or she will be your victim after the last line of this story. Make sure that he or she has a robust temperament.

Tell the following story:

> *Once there was a woman who went out to pick beans, and she found a hairy toe. She took the hairy toe home with her, and late that night, she seemed to hear a voice crying:* [ghostly voice] *'Who's got my hairy toe? Where's my hairy toe?'*
>
> *The woman scrooched down under the covers and, at that very moment, the wind appeared to hit the house, SMOOSH! The wind rumbled as if some big animal was trying to get in. The voice had come nearer now, and it said:* [threatening voice] *'Who's got my hairy toe? Where's my hairy toe?'*
>
> *The woman scrooched further down under the covers and she heard the door creak. 'Creak, creak, creak', it said – and then the voice:* [almost silent voice, but they can tell what you are saying because of the repetition, and because of your vocalization] *'Who's got my hairy toe? Where's my hairy toe . . .'*
>
> [Take a long pause, as long as you can. Then say this to the victim, as loud as you dare . . .]
> *'YOU'VE GOT IT!'*

Was [the child who sat next to you] frightened? Yes, of course – but not for long. And other things that happen to us may frighten us, but it doesn't always last for long.

Tell the children about things that have frightened you in your lifetime:

o The dark
o Crowds
o Loneliness.

What has frightened them? Collect responses.

Music: 'Fingal's Cave' by Mendelssohn.

Preparation: A glass of water.

Tell the children: 'Here are some statements about water. I want you to listen to them, think and then decide whether they are true or false.' Make it clear they should think first! Impose a few seconds silence before hands may be raised.

○ Camels store fat in their humps, and water in their stomachs.
○ The Sahara Desert in Africa is about the same size as the USA.
○ 70% of the earth's surface is water.
○ 98% of that water is salty, so humans can't drink it.
○ 90% of water on earth that humans *can* drink is underground.
○ On average, a human being drinks 50,000 litres of water in a lifetime.
○ Humans can live for weeks without food, but only a few days without water.

True or false? Do a rough count of hands for each one. Tell the children: 'They are all true.' Some problems:

○ The earth is getting warmer and the level of the seas and oceans is rising.
○ Pollution from factories is flowing straight into rivers.
○ Sewage is flowing into the sea.
○ Chemicals used on the land are washed by rain into our water supply.

'What can we do? We should not let taps run while we clean our teeth. Can you think of anything else?'

Music: Something solemn.

Here's the last story about Hannah and her Grandfather.

Hannah and her Grandfather loved each other. When Hannah was small, her Grandfather had been able to play football with her in the winter and cricket in the summer. The lawn was worn bare in patches where Hannah had batted and bowled in the summer and saved Grandfather's shots in the winter.

But now Grandfather was too old to play. He mostly sat in his armchair, reading. Sometimes he read to Hannah.

They loved each other. They also loved cacti. Grandfather had been collecting them for many years and, when she was seven, Hannah had started to help collecting and looking after them.

She loved helping Grandfather to re-pot the ones that needed more soil and more space for their roots. When she took them out of the old pot, the roots were all tangled and squashed. She thought of them in their new bigger pots, and imagined them saying, 'Ah, that's better, I can stretch out now . . .'

Their little sun room had shelves full of cacti. There were tiny ones that grew a little bigger as each year went by. There were knobbly, yellow ones. And there was one that flowered in great pinkish-red flames every winter. When Hannah touched the prickles on the cacti, they were strong.

Hannah loved the names and often whispered them to herself: 'Hedgehog cactus, silver torch cactus, sunset cactus, old man cactus . . .'

Hannah's parents used to watch Grandfather and the young girl pottering in the sun room, and smile broad, bright smiles. Sometimes they took photographs and stuck them all on the wall of the sun room.

But the old man was getting weaker and weaker. Some days, he only got out of bed for a few hours. Then, Hannah and her Grandfather would read to each other in the bedroom, the old man lying in the bed, the girl lying on it.

The doctor came to see the old man sometimes, and to talk to Hannah's parents.

One day the old man didn't get up at all. Hannah knew that he was going to die.

Then the house was quiet for a few days.

After her Grandfather had died, Hannah looked at the cacti in a different way. They were sad now. But she was glad of them. She learned how to re-pot them by herself. Her parents used to watch her in the sun room, with smiles on their faces, not broad and bright, but sad.

I will never forget Grandfather, Hannah thought. He lives on in the sun room where the cacti go on growing, and where we have put the photographs, and he lives on in my head. She whispered the names to herself again: 'Hedgehog cactus, silver torch cactus, sunset cactus, old man cactus . . .'

And at Christmas that year one of the cacti shot out its flamey flowers brighter and larger than ever.

FS

Ask the children:

○ Where is Grandfather now?
○ What will Hannah have to remember her Grandfather by?
○ Has anyone any happy memories of a grandfather/ grandmother/great-grandfather/great-grandmother?

Music: Same as for Idea 82.

'Yesterday, we heard about Hannah's Grandfather's death. I have a memory of – [a story of your own here about a relative will win children round, because they will appreciate your honesty, and knowing something important about you]. Who has happy memories of someone in their family who has died?'

You might prefer to meet the children who are going to speak before the assembly. I'd take a risk myself.

One boy told the school about a grandfather who had been a sailor and who used to sing:

Potatoes and gravy
Potatoes and gravy
That's the stuff you get in the navy.
I'm happy by gum
When I'm tight as a drum
Packed up with
Potatoes and gravy.

Another child remembered how her Grandad used to give her sweets when her parents weren't looking.

One girl wrote this:

I remember the snow on the window ledge, and the
holly berries falling off. The birds scuttling around and
looking for food. Grandad and Nana holding hands
and, on my Mum's lap, me asleep with my dummy in
my mouth.

These memories will stimulate others.

Meditation
Ask the children to say this after you, phrase by phrase:

God be in my head, and in my understanding;
God be in mine eyes, and in my looking;
God be in my mouth, and in my speaking;
God be in my heart, and in my thinking;
God be at mine end, and my departing.

Every now and then, it is good to have an assembly that surprises the children.

Empty a tin of something pleasant that the children would eat (fruit, beans, etc.) and wash the tin and remove the label. Take a cat-food label and stick it around the tin. Make up a concoction of chocolate bars mixed with orange jelly. Cut the chocolate up and make the jelly thick. It will look like cat food. Put the mix into the tin.

Pretend that you were late for school, missed breakfast and grabbed what you thought was a tin of fruit (say) on the way out of the house. You arrived at school and opened the tin and only then did you realize that it was a tin of cat food. Put a fork in and lift some out and make as if you are going to vomit at the thought of eating it. Let the children have a look and really ham up how disgusting it is. (Don't let them smell it.)

Then say that you are really hungry and take a tiny bite. The children will start shrieking. Then take a massive bite – the shriek will be even worse. Get a friendly colleague up to have a bite. The kids will continue to go crazy.

Then get some child volunteers up and ask them to eat some. It is amazing to watch their faces change – from almost gagging at the thought of it, to loving it because it tastes really good.

Then hit them with the moral. Just because it looks brown and nasty and it is in a cat food tin – which signals nasty for us – it isn't necessarily so. Tell them a story along these lines: 'My friend had the ugliest dog you could imagine [describe – one ear missing, eyes tiny and crooked, etc.]. Tell them how you hated it on sight. And then how it turned out to be the most loving dog you had ever known.

Preparation: Helen Keller died on 1 June 1968, so this, her anniversary, would be a suitable date for this assembly. As would 27 June, her birthday.

It would be useful to have (and I have always found them easy to obtain from the local branch of the Royal National Institute for the Blind) some Braille sheets. Some children could be brought out to the front to feel them.

Here is Helen Keller's story.

In 1880 a girl was born in Alabama in the USA. Just before she was two years old, she became ill. When she got better, her parents found that she was both deaf and blind. Soon she became mute: she didn't speak.

When she was seven, she was wild. All the things she couldn't do frustrated her. She couldn't hear what her friends said, nor say anything to them. And, of course, she couldn't see anything in the world, except the dark inside her mind.

Her mother and father found a young woman called Annie Sullivan to teach their daughter. One day Helen was running wildly about the garden. She knew it so well with her sense of touch that her blindness didn't stop her running. Annie hated the wildness: the movement and the animal sounds. She grabbed hold of Helen's hand and stuck it under the water pump. The shock of the cold water made Helen go silent for a moment. In the silence, Annie printed on Helen's palm the letters W. A. T. E. R.

A light shone in Helen's mind. She began to connect the sudden chill of the water with the letters W. A. T. E. R.

Annie was a clever woman. She pulled Helen about the garden, rubbing her hand, first, on the bark of a tree, and then writing T.R.E.E. on her hand. Then G.R.A.S.S., E.A.R.T.H. and P.U.M.P. And, for the first time, Helen knew that words lived for things, and that, although she could neither see nor hear, it would be possible for her to learn those words. She could come to understand the world she lived in, and to make it a bright place, rather than a dark one.

125

Helen became a teacher and lecturer, travelling the world to help people who were blind, deaf and mute like herself. She wrote books, and someone wrote a book about her. It was made into a film.

Suggest: We are all blind in one way or another. We can see nature, or pictures, but not the beauty in them. We are deaf too. We can hear the sound of a blackbird singing, but not hear its loveliness.

Meditation

Sunlight on the bright pavement. A wood pigeon going on and on, as if forever. Onions frying on a Friday evening. The crunch of an apple as I bite.

O God, help us to look at the world until it hurts, and to listen to its sounds, and to smell its smells, and to taste its tastes. Amen.

Preparation: A shopping list with a variety of things on it.

'Everyone makes a shopping list. Here's mine from last Saturday . . .' [Read a shopping list.]

Tell the children that some people make a list of all the things they've got to do on a certain day. 'What have you got to do today?' Collect some suggestions. Write them on the OHP.

'Let's make some lists about other things. Things I like, for example.' One girl in another school where I taught wrote this list:

> *Pretty girls, flying doves, lovely poems, bold men, fizzy drinks, summer holidays and lots of friends.*

Ask the children for some lists of things they like. They should close their eyes first, and have a good think.

Then, extend the idea. Ask for lists, but with this difference: each object on the list should have the word 'because . . .' after it:

○ Horses running, because they are fast
○ Maths, because of the sums
○ Smells of Scottish air, because I come from Scotland
○ Making things, because it is gluey.

Now make a list called 'Things my friend does for me . . .' Start them off:

○ Takes me to football matches
○ Looks after me when I am sad.

And another called 'Things I believe. . .'. For example, 'I believe I should be kind to friends . . ., I believe my team is the best . . .'.

How about a list of things that have gone wrong today? And, more importantly, a list of things that have gone right?

Sometimes, assemblies should simply be light and enjoyable, like this one. Playground rhymes are about the democracy of metre and rhyme: they are beautiful things that everyone – not just those we think of as 'real poets' – are entitled to.

Tell the children: 'Many people believe that you first come across poetry when you open a poetry book, maybe at school, maybe at home. This isn't true. You come across poetry long before that.'

'Maybe in the cradle, in the playground, in the street. Your parents said, for example, "This little piggy went to market / This little piggy stayed at home . . ."' Ask the children to finish this rhyme.

Here are some rhymes from schools from all around the world. A globe or a large map of the world would be useful here. You could point to where the rhymes come from.

1

Enny feeny figgery feg
Deely dyly ham and egg
Calico back and stony rock
Arlum barlum BASH!

2

Hokey pokey winky wum
How do you like your taties done?
Snip snap snorum
Hi popalorum
Kate go scratch it
You are OUT!

3

1,2,3,
Mother caught a flea.
She put it in the teapot
and made a pot of tea.

The flea jumped out,
Mother gave a shout
And in comes the bobby
With his shirt hanging out.

4

What's your name? Mary Jane
Where d'you live? Down the grid
What number? Cucumber
What house? Pig scouse.

The above rhymes come from the UK, the first two from
Scotland and the last from Liverpool, where the people
are sometimes called 'scousers'.

These three are from the Caribbean:

1

Order in the court
The judge is eating beans,
His wife is in the bathtub
Shooting submarines.

2

Clap hands for your mammy
Till your daddy come
Bringing cakes and sugarplum
Give baby some.

3

Abna Babna
Lady Snee
Ocean potion
Sugar and tea
Potato roast and English toast
And out goes she.

Two more from England:

1

Ibble obble
black bobble
ibble obble out
Granny put her knickers on
inside out.

Stephanie bom bephanie
sticka lephanie
fi fephanie
fi fephanie
sticka lephanie
that's how you spell Stephanie.

This last one can be adapted to any name, but beware of 'Martin'.

Collect some rhymes. Be prepared for mild ribaldry . . . All over the world, children are collecting, making up, singing and saying rhymes. Many of them are different versions of what is essentially the same rhyme. We are all human beings, and we have more in common that we have that is different!

Preparation: It would add to this assembly if you could show the children a symbol for each religion: cross, crescent moon, Star of David, etc.

A glimpse at religions. This is an assembly geared towards Key Stage 2 children.

Read these quotations to the children. Which is the odd one out?

In the beginning God created the heaven and the earth. . . (The Bible: Genesis 1:1, Judaism)

There is no Hindu. There is no Muslim. I am a brother to all who love God, and all lovers of God are brothers together. (Guru Nanak, Sikhism)

God gives you life and He gives you death; and God sees very well all that you do. (Qur'an: Sura 3, Islam)

Three things cannot be hidden: the sun, the moon and the truth. (The Buddha)

O God we praise you with our thoughts as the sun praises you in the morning. (Hindu prayer, Hinduism)

Blessed are the peacemakers: for they shall be called the children of God. (The Bible: Matthew 5:9, Christianity)

Which is the odd one out? It's the Buddhist prayer. This prayer does not mention God. Buddhism is not a theistic religion. You can be an atheist Buddhist.

What do they all have in common? What are the keywords? According to me they are: God (apart from the Buddhist quote), brother (and sister), love, truth, praise and peacemakers.

Here is another quotation from the Jewish scriptures:

'To every thing there is a season, and a time to every purpose under the heaven.' (The Bible: Ecclesiastes 3:1, Judaism and Christianity)

Meditation
Now it is the time to be brothers and sisters, to search for the truth and to make peace among ourselves.

131

Ask the children: 'How many different kinds of building can you think of? Houses, blocks of flats, schools, hospitals, shops, surgeries, huts, churches, mosques, synagogues . . .'

Make a list down one side of an OHP or whiteboard. Ask the children: 'What is the purpose of each of these buildings?'

Draw a line from each kind of building to its purpose(s). To live in, to learn in, to make friends in, to store in, to be cured in, to help other people be cured, to spend money in, to worship in, etc. . . .

What are the component parts of a building? Study the room you are in now: walls, roof, windows, etc.

Ask the children to close their eyes and think of a building that they know. Ask some of the children to describe the building they have been thinking of. What is the most important part of a building? The roof? The walls? No. It's something that we can't see. It's something strong. It is the foundations.

Our lives have foundations. There are rocks under everything we do: the love we feel for our families, our carers and our friends. The beliefs we hold, in God, in humankind, in freedom.

Here's a story Jesus told:

Whoever listens to my sayings, and does them, is like a man who builds his house on a rock. The rain came down, the floods came, the winds blew and beat on the house, and it didn't fall.

Why?

Because it was built on rock.

Whoever listens to my sayings, and does not do them, is like a man who builds his house on sand. The rain came down, the floods came, the winds blew and beat on the house, and it fell, and great was the fall of it.

Why?

Because it was built on sand. (St Matthew 7)

Meditation

Think in the silence about the people whom we love, and who love us. And about other things to which we must be true. These are the rocks on which our life-house is built.

Preparation: For this assembly you need either large books of reproductions (available cheaply at remainder shops) or, preferably, some large-scale reproductions. Better still, use some original artwork.

Show the children a picture, and ask them questions along the following lines. These questions refer to Seurat's painting *Bathers at Asnieres*, so this assembly is a template for any assembly you might lead on a favourite picture. 'Look hard at the picture for a minute.'

Questions about technique:

○ Tell me where on the canvas the colours are lighter? Darker?
○ Can you see how Seurat has applied the paint?
○ Point out the hazy quality of the picture. How has Seurat done this?

Questions about content:

○ What are these people doing?
○ Describe what they are wearing.
○ Can you imagine them moving much? (They are, in fact, very still.)
○ Tell me about the background.
○ There are lots of everyday things in this picture. Can you list them?
○ One boy is drinking from the river. What would the water be like?

The point here is the smoking chimney in the background. The scene is not the idyllic one that casual observers of the picture, and even some serious critics, usually assume.

Finally, use metre sticks to show how large the picture is: 3 metres by 2!

If you are in London, the original is easily accessible, at the National Gallery in Trafalgar Square.

Ask the children to find a picture they like, and to discuss it with their friends.

THE CARETAKER

Preparation: For this assembly you need the caretaker! And some of his or her equipment: brooms, buffer, vacuum cleaner.

Interview him or her:

○ Sometimes caretakers are called 'Custodians' or 'Site managers'. Which do you prefer, and why?
○ What did you do for a job before you became a caretaker?
○ Why did you leave that job?
○ What is the best part of your work?
○ And the worst?
○ Can you show us how the buffer works, please.
○ What is it for?
○ What could we do to make your job easier?

George Herbert, a seventeenth-century poet, wrote: 'Who sweeps a room, as for [God's] laws, / Makes that and the action fine.'

He meant this: every job we do can be done well and to the glory of God.

This assembly could be replicated (with appropriate changes) for the secretary, the crossing patrol, the cook, the dinner ladies . . . and anyone usually perceived as being on the edge of school life. It could be followed by the children producing drawings of the caretaker at work.

For this assembly, act out this playlet with a colleague:

> COLLEAGUE *enters, sits at desk*
> *Long pause*
> YOU *sitting at another desk, writing*: You're late.
> Again.
> COLLEAGUE: I know. Traffic terrible. Pass me
> that pen.
> YOU: It's mine.
> COLLEAGUE *reaches over you, almost touching
> you, gets the pen*: So? Are you using it?
> YOU *look furiously at* COLLEAGUE. *Your mobile
> rings.* YOU *answer, loudly*: Hello sweetheart . . . Yup
> . . . yeah . . . no beans, though. Hate beans. Yeah
> . . . loads of spuds, though, roasted. Can't stand
> boiled spuds . . . yeah . . . yeah . . . see you later . . .
> *During this* COLLEAGUE *has been getting visibly
> angrier and angrier.* YOU *and* COLLEAGUE *get
> up to out of the door, together, and get stuck in the
> doorway . . . You stare furiously at each other.*

Ask the children: 'What did we do wrong? Or not do
right?'

Another version:

> COLLEAGUE *enters, sits at desk*: Morning John.
> Good night last night?
> YOU *sitting at desk, writing, look up with a smile*:
> Yes, watched *The Bill.* Wrote a few emails to
> friends. You?
> COLLEAGUE: Oh not bad. Went swimming. We
> must go out for coffee together some day.
> YOU: Love to. You're a fraction late, by the way.
> COLLEAGUE: I know. All my fault. Slept too
> long. Won't happen again. Sorry. Could I borrow
> your pen?
> YOU: That's OK. And, yes, of course. Here.
> *Your mobile rings. You go out of the room, talking
> quietly on the phone. When you come back, more polite
> chat as you work.* YOU *and* COLLEAGUE *get up to
> go out of the door.*

YOU: After you, Caroline.
COLLEAGUE: Thank you!

'What did we do better?' Collect responses, among them, almost certainly:

○ You used 'Please' and 'Thank you'.
○ You apologized.
○ You showed an interest in each other's lives.
○ Colleague didn't make excuses about being late, but accepted her responsibility.

'Why are manners important? They tell the other person that he/she exists, that he/she matters. What polite things can we do around the school to each other?' Collect some answers.

Have children in the other years prepare 'presents' for Year 6 – a class poem, a set of pictures, a song, a play, a dance – and offer them in the assembly. This should be carefully prepared and rehearsed in terms of the rules in Idea 16 of this book.

Then the leavers read pieces they've written about memories of their time at school. Trigger this with a memory of your own about:

○ Your schooldays
○ Coming to this school
○ A Christmas play
○ A school visit
○ A teacher who has since left.

You or a teacher should think of a (happy!) memory about each leaver. Here are some memories from children in other schools. They were based on Thomas Hood's widely anthologized poem 'I remember, I remember':

○ I remember my first day at school. My parents disappeared around a corner, leaving me with unknown faces staring at me. Then I felt all grown up. I had my Barbie lunchbox, and Kiera's Ribena leaked all through. [Details are everything here: that Ribena, for example.]
○ I remember getting into trouble with Mr ___ and I had to stand outside his room all dinner time.

Meditation

> *Dear God,*
> *We thank our leavers for their pasts with us, and pray*
> *for their safety and joy in their futures without us.*
> *Amen.*

WHEN A TEACHER LEAVES

For this assembly, which should happen before your colleague leaves, you need to find an excuse for him or her not to be there.

Tell the children about a teacher at your school when you were a child. It must be a teacher you were fond of. For example, I remember an English teacher who gave me a book of poems when I left. I still have it on my shelves to this day. He'd seen that I loved poetry. I would like to say to him now: 'You sowed the seed of my poetry life with that present.'

Ask the children to think of things they would like to say to Mr ___ or Ms ___, who is leaving school soon. To trigger responses, talk about the teacher's main interests: sport, the school productions at Christmas, music, poetry, maths . . . Ask the children to write the sentences down, to be presented to the teacher on his or her last day.

Music: 'Summertime' from George and Ira Gershwin's *Porgy and Bess*.

Read this list poem to the children, emphasizing the alliteration (l's and b's in the first stanza, for example) and assonance (the 'aw' in line one of the second):

Lie in bed late
lounging and lolling about
Eat eggs and bacon
for breakfast at eleven

Sprawl on the lawn
with a long glass of lemonade
Eat salad and seafood
Travel the town T-shirted

greeting mates
grinning with freedom Bowl
Bash those bails down
Belt a leather ball

bouncing to the boundary bounce bounce
Bring
a take-away home
parathas and puppadoms

Talk about treats
sunlight through trees and sand
Sleep in deep silence between sheets
Dream

FS

Read it again, asking the children to put their hands up at each example of alliteration.

Tell the children some of the things you will do on the first day of the summer holidays. Ask them for some of the things they will do (include the teachers and learning support assistants, of course). Ask the children to go back to class and write a list poem about what they will do.

Compile with the children a list of things to *be* during the summer holidays, starting with 'safe' and 'helpful'.

Dealing with special days

Throughout the year, death should be prepared for. Like it or not, we are in its presence all the time. You could begin this preparation with a withered pot plant. It was alive, but now it's dead. And you could continue with the deaths of animals.

Here's a poem that introduces this subject in a painless way:

DANIEL'S RABBIT

> *The rabbit wasn't old*
> *but still he's dead.*
> *He thinks he's a dog*
> *Aunt Alison said,*
> *the way he would sniff*
> *and follow you or lie*
> *stretched out on your bed.*
> *But now when I whisper his name*
> *he doesn't twitch at all*
> *and Grandad's going to bury him*
> *by the garden shed*
> *and I never learned*
> *how to pick him up*
> *and now he's dead.*

FS

Ask the children for memories of pets.

When the infinitely more tragic issue of the death of human beings arises, it simply has to be addressed.

When Justin, who was eight, died after an illness that had lasted about ten months, the children in his class were asked to write down their favourite memories of what Justin used to do. They read these to the rest of the school, having practised, and remembering the lessons in Idea 16 about speaking clearly, using good breathing and so on.

His teacher read sentences from a record card: 'Justin is beginning to read with great expression', 'Justin is learning the recorder, and applies himself well' and so on. Then everyone closed their eyes, and remembered Justin. And sang his favourite hymn.

Music: Something sombre.

This isn't so much an assembly as a note about talking about disasters.

I was in a school in the south of England when something unspeakable happened. It happened some 400 miles away in what was, to these children (and to me), the far north. The news broke at teatime. A class of children and their teacher had been massacred in the school hall. It was so unspeakable that teachers never mention the perpetrator's name.

The next day I was working in the school again. As I arrived, I asked the headteacher what she was going to say to the chidren about the news. She said: 'Nothing.'

Obviously, there is a chasm as huge as the journey from Earth to Pluto between the everyday experience of most schools and the experience of violence in the world. But in this news story, that chasm was tragically bridged. And the school in the south must do something about it. One idea is to bring in a copy of the day's paper to school, and to talk about the event.

As I write, New Orleans is recovering from Hurricane Katrina. When discussing this in an assembly, you might play some New Orleans jazz. And on other occasions play music from the part of the world currently affected by a disaster.

Distinguish between:

○ Natural disasters – Some call these 'Acts of God'. 'What do you think of that?' Is a famine, hurricane or earthquake, an act of God? Or is it human-made?
○ Human-made disasters.

With the first example, given above, the children need a basic reassurance that, despite whatever they have seen on their televisions the night before, 'We will do all we can to look after you.'

Ask the children to say the following, after you, phrase by phrase:

To every thing
there is a season
and a time

143

for every purpose
under heaven:
A time to be born,
and a time to die;
a time to plant,
and a time to pluck up that which is planted;
A time to kill,
and a time to heal;
a time to break down,
and a time to build up;
A time to weep,
and a time to laugh;
a time to mourn,
and a time to dance;
A time to love,
and a time to hate;
a time of war,
and a time of peace.

Ecclesiastes 3:1–8

When is it right to hate? When you are hating things, beliefs, deeds. Not people.

Someone at your school will decide when a fire drill takes place. It is a good idea if, at least once a year, this is during an assembly. Obviously, the following will take place outside in the playground, or wherever you have evacuated the children. It is a chance to reiterate rules about safety.

After an evacuation the children will feel strange to be outside during school time. Use that strangeness. Ask the children to look around: 'What can you see? The grass moving in the wind, the trees swaying with birds on branches, birds in flight (notice how they don't accelerate: they take off at the speed at which they continue), the cars moving down the road, the clouds drifting across the sky. Can you see any animals? Breathe in, deeply. What can you smell? Listen, with your eyes closed. What can you hear?'

Go back into your classrooms and write, draw, look up in encyclopaedias everything you have seen, heard and smelt. This is God's world. Celebrate it.

FIRE DRILL

CELEBRATION

In many schools, the final assembly of the week is a celebration of the work the children have done; what American teachers call a 'show-and-tell'. Again, this isn't an assembly, but some basic rules for how to do it.

○ Vary the contents. Cover as many curriculum areas as possible in each assembly. There should be English, Science, Mathematics, History, Geography, etc.

○ Keep the contributions short.

○ Make sure there is a visual element to each assembly, not just words.

○ A teacher should make a contribution.

○ The rules in Idea 16 should be repeated until they are part of the air the school breathes.

Read the children some endings from famous children's books, and ask them to identify them. Then ask:

o Do you remember the first assembly? I asked you about how you begin things, like life, or a day.
o How do you end a day? A cup of cocoa, a story, a sleep?

What do we have to do when something bigger than a day, like a school year, ends? We have to say goodbye. We have to look forward to the future. We have to remember some of the lessons we have learnt in our assemblies:

o We are made in the image of God: we can make beautiful things.
o Sometimes life will demand that we are brave: braver, perhaps, than we feel like being. Like Daniel or the Indian Prince.
o Sometimes life will demand that we overcome great problems, as Helen Keller did.
o And, certainly, life will take someone from us whom we love, as Grandfather was taken away from Hannah.
o Sometimes life will demand that we rejoice in the beautiful things in our world: nature, buildings, paintings and music.
o Always, life will demand that we are kind to our friends, and loyal to them.

SOME COMMON NAMES, WITH THEIR MEANINGS

Key: A = Arabic, AS = Anglo-Saxon, Gk = Greek, L = Latin, H = Hebrew

Alice, Alison: truth (Gk)

Amanda, Amy: loved one (L)

Andrew: a man (Gk). Also Carl and Charles: man (Teutonic)

Ann, Anna, Anne, Hannah: grace (Gk, from H)

Benjamin: son of the right hand (H)

Chloe: green and tender shoot (Gk)

Christopher: carrier of Christ (Gk)

Clare: clear (L)

Daniel: God is my judge (H)

David: man after God's own heart (H)

Douglas: from a dark stream (Scot)

Edward: guard (AS)

Felicity: happiness (L)

George: earth-worker (Gk)

Helen: bright (Gk)

Ian, Ivan, Jack, Jane, Joanna, John: grace of the Lord (H)

James: heel (H)

Jonathan: the Lord's gift (H)

Jordan: descender (H)

Joseph: he shall add (H)

Joshua: salvation (H) (= Jesus)

Katharine, Catherine, Kate, etc: pure (Gk)

Laurence, Laura, Lauren: from the laurel tree (L)

Leila: darkness, night (A)

Mary, Maria, Marian, Miriam: bitterness (H)

Matthew: gift of the Lord (H)

Mohammad (A) is, of course, the name of the prophet

Nicholas: victory of the people (Gk)

Paul, Paula: small (L)

Peter: a rock (Gk)

Rachel: ewe (H)

Rebecca: snare (H)

Robert: bright flame (AS)

Sophy: knowledge or wisdom (Gk)

Zoe: life (Gk)